THE ULTIMATE
CUISINART AIR FRYER OVEN
COOKBOOK FOR BEGINNERS

1500-Day Simple & Amazing Cuisinart Air Fryer Recipes to Help You
Start Air Fry, Toast, Bake, Broil, Grill, and More

Constance Jakubowski

Contents

1 Introduction

2 Fundamentals of Cuisinart Air Fryer Toaster Oven

9 4-Week Meal Plan

11 Chapter 1 Breakfast

22   Chapter 2 Vegetables and Sides

34   Chapter 3 Poultry

77 Chapter 7 Desserts

87 Conclusion

88 Appendix 1 Measurement Conversion Chart

89 Appendix 2 Air Fryer Cooking Chart

90 Appendix 3 Recipes Index

Introduction

The new Cuisinart Air Fryer Toaster Oven is an advanced multi-functional cooking appliance that works on hot air circulation technology. It can fry, bake, roast, and broil with little to no oil. With seven functions, it can do everything from toast bread and reheat leftovers to roast a whole chicken. The capacity is large enough to fit six slices of toast or a 12-inch pizza. The unit comes with a baking pan, an air fryer basket, and a recipe book. Air frying requires no preheating, so it's ready to cook as soon as you load the food in.

It is a versatile appliance that can be used for air frying, toasting, broiling, and convection baking. It features a powerful 1800-watt heating element that ensures even cooking, while the four-quart capacity allows you to cook large meals. The digital control panel makes it easy to select the desired cooking function, and the unit comes with a fry basket, baking pan, and broil rack. It is an all-in-one appliance that will make a great addition to your kitchen.

The Cuisinart Air Fryer Toaster Oven Cookbook is the perfect guide for anyone who wants to learn how to use their air fryer oven to make delicious, healthy meals. Featuring over 100 recipes specifically designed for air fryer ovens, this cookbook covers everything from breakfast dishes to desserts. If you want to make a quick and easy weeknight meal or want to simply impress your friends and family with a gourmet dish, the Cuisinart Air Fryer Oven Cookbook has you covered. In addition to step-by-step instructions, each recipe includes tips on how to get the best results, as well as mouthwatering photos of the finished dish.

Whereas the Cuisinart Air Fryer Toaster Oven is a new and versatile appliance that is used for a variety of cooking tasks. Air frying uses less oil than traditional frying methods, so it's a healthier option. It has a wide range of temperatures, so you can easily cook your food to perfection. The appliance also has a built-in self-clean function, so you don't have to worry about messy clean-up. And if you're looking for a toaster oven that can do it all, the Cuisinart Air Fryer Toaster Oven is the perfect choice.

What is Cuisinart Air Fryer Toaster Oven?

Cuisinart Air Fryer Toaster Oven is a kitchen appliance that combines the functions of an air fryer, toaster oven, and convection oven. It is manufactured by the American home appliance brand Cuisinart. The product was first introduced in 2018 and quickly gained popularity due to its compact size, multiple functions, and ability to cook food quickly and evenly. The Air Fryer Toaster Oven uses hot air to fry food, eliminating the need for oil or butter. It also has a built-in toaster oven function that can be used to toast bread, bagels, and other pastries. In addition, the Air Fryer Toaster Oven has a convection feature that circulates hot air throughout the oven, cooking food more evenly and quickly.

Benefits of Using it

Who doesn't love fried foods? The crispy, salty goodness is hard to resist. But fried foods are also notoriously unhealthy, loaded with fat and calories. That's where the Cuisinart Air Fryer Toaster Oven comes in. This innovative appliance uses cutting-edge technology to fry foods with little or no oil, making it a healthier alternative to traditional frying methods. And because it's a toaster oven, it can also be used to bake, broil and toast, making it a versatile addition to any kitchen. No wonder the Cuisinart Air Fryer Toaster Oven is becoming so popular. It's the perfect way to enjoy delicious fried foods without all the guilt.

When it comes to kitchen appliances, the Cuisinart Air Fryer Toaster Oven is one of the best. This handy appliance can not only toast and air fry your food, but it also has a host of other functions that make it a must-have for any kitchen. Here are 15 benefits of owning a Cuisinart Air Fryer Toaster Oven:

It's multifunctional

The Cuisinart Air Fryer Toaster Oven can do more than just toast and air fry your food. It can also bake, broil, warm, and reheat your meals. This makes it perfect for those who want to save time in the kitchen.

Cooks food evenly

The Cuisinart Air Fryer Toaster Oven uses convection cooking for the purpose of circulating hot air around food, cooking it evenly on all sides. This prevents hot spots that can cause uneven cooking and burned food.

Retains nutrients

Because the Cuisinart Air Fryer Toaster Oven cooks food quickly and evenly, it helps to retain more of the nutrients than other cooking methods. This is especially beneficial for foods that are high in vitamins and minerals.

Reduces fat and calories

The Cuisinart Air Fryer Toaster Oven uses little or no oil to

cook food. This reduces the fat and calorie content of meals, making them healthier overall.

Can accommodate large quantities

This Cuisinart Air Fryer Toaster Oven is large enough to accommodate large quantities of food. This is ideal for cooking for a crowd or meal prepping for the week ahead.

Lightweight

The Cuisinart Air Fryer Toaster Oven weighs just over 10 pounds, making it easy to move around as needed.

It comes with a removable drip and crumb tray

The drip tray makes it easy to deal with the food and you don't have to worry about oil splatters when you're cooking with this appliance. Whereas the crumb tray makes cleanup quick and easy after each use. Simply remove the tray and empty it

into the trash or compost bin.

It comes with an instruction booklet

This booklet provides step-by-step instructions on how to use the different functions of the Cuisinart Air Fryer Toaster Oven, as well as helpful tips on how to get the best results when cooking with an air fryer.

One-year warranty

While buying the Cuisinart Air Fryer Toaster Oven you get a one-year warranty that ensures that you will get help from customer service if you experience any problems with your appliance within the first year of ownership, taking away any worry about making a long-term investment.

Easy to clean

It has a nonstick interior that makes cleanup quick and easy. There is also no need to worry about oil splatters with this appliance.

Economical

This Oven is an economical appliance to use because it doesn't require oil or butter for cooking. This saves money on groceries and promotes healthy eating habits.

Durable

The Cuisinart Air Fryer Toaster Oven is made from high-quality materials that make it highly durable and long lasting. This ensures that you get years of use from this appliance without having to replace it frequently.

Attractive design

The Cuisinart Air Fryer Oven has a sleek and modern design that looks great in any kitchen décor scheme."

Versatile

As mentioned before, the Cuisinart Air Fryer Toaster Oven can do more than just fry food. It can also bake, broil, and toast, making it a versatile addition to any kitchen.

Safe

The Cuisinart Air Fryer Toaster Oven has an automatic shut-off feature that prevents it from overheating. This makes it a safe appliance to use in the kitchen.

Reasonable Price

Considering all the Cuisinart Air Fryer Toaster Oven offers, the price is quite affordable, making it a great value for your money.

ETL certified

The Cuisinart Air Fryer Toaster Oven meets high safety standards, giving you peace of mind when using it in your home.

Energy efficient

The Cuisinart Air Fryer Toaster Oven is energy-efficient. It uses 70% less energy than a conventional oven, so you can save money on your energy bills.

It comes with six accessory pieces

These include an oven rack, an AirFry basket, a baking pan, a broiling pan, and a recipe book full of delicious recipes specifically designed for use with an Cuisinart Air Fryer Toaster Oven.

Excellent customer service

If you have any problems with your Cuisinart Air Fryer Toaster Oven, simply contact customer service for assistance. The company's friendly and helpful representatives will be more than happy to help you troubleshoot any issues you may be having or answer any questions you may have about the product.

The Features of It

Some features of the Cuisinart Air Fryer Oven that make it a unique and useful appliance are:

Power Indicator

The Cuisinart Air Fryer Oven is a unique and innovative kitchen appliance. Not only does it have the ability to air fry your food, but it also has a built-in toaster oven. This allows you to cook multiple items at once, making it a perfect appliance for those who love to entertain. One of the best features of the Cuisinart Air Fryer Toaster Oven is the Power On Light Indicator. This light will turn on and remain lit when the oven is in use. This is a great safety feature that allows you to see if the oven is still on, even if you're not in the kitchen. It's also a helpful way to know when your food is done cooking. The Power On Light Indicator is just one of the many reasons why the Cuisinart Air Fryer Toaster Oven is an amazing kitchen appliance.

Timer Dial

This dial can be used to set the desired cooking time for all

Temperature Dial

The Cuisinart Air Fryer Toaster Oven comprises of an Oven Temperature Dial that allows you to set the desired temperature for your food. This is an important feature as it helps to ensure that your food is cooked evenly and at the right temperature. The dial also has an indicator light that lets you know when the oven is preheated and ready to use.

Function Dial

The Function Dial is used to select the desired cooking method, and the corresponding settings will be automatically applied. For example, if you select the Toast setting, the oven will preheat to the ideal temperature for toasting bread. The AirFry setting is perfect for creating crispy foods without using oil, and the Convection Bake setting can be used for baking cakes and cookies. Whether you want to warm up leftovers or bake a dessert, the Cuisinart Air Fryer Toaster Oven can help you get the job done.

Light Button

The Cuisinart Air Fryer Oven has a light button that turns on the interior oven light. This is a highly convenient feature that allows you to see the food as it cooks. The light will turn off automatically when the oven is not in use. Please note that it comprises of a bulb-saver feature allowing the light to work only when the oven is being used. The light will not work whenever power is off. This is a safety feature that prevents

functions except the Toast function. Once the desired time has been set, the unit will power on and begin the cooking cycle. When the time is complete, the unit will power off. This feature is particularly useful for ensuring that food is cooked evenly and thoroughly. In addition, it allows users to free up their hands for other tasks while the appliance is in use.

the bulb from overheating.

Safety Auto Off Door Switch

This oven has a safety auto Off switch that cuts off power when the oven door is opened. This feature helps to prevent accidents and ensures that the appliance is used safely.

AirFryer Basket

With the AirFryer Basket, you can maximize your cooking

results by using it in conjunction with the AirFry function. The basket is designed to nest within the baking pan, so it's always ready to work when you need it. And since it's made of non-stick material, cleanup is a breeze.

Oven Rack

The Air Fryer Toaster Oven has a removable oven rack that can be used in two positions. Position 1 (bottom) is for conventional baking and browning, while Position 2 (top) is 50% stopped so the rack only comes halfway out of the oven, ideal for dehydrating or keeping food warm. The rack can be removed from Position 2 by first lifting the front of the rack and then sliding it out. When not in use, the oven rack should be stored in a safe, dry place. For best results, follow the instructions in the manual when using the Cuisinart Air Fryer Toaster Oven.

Baking Pan

The Toaster Oven comes with a Baking Pan/Drip Tray for your convenience. This pan can be used alone when baking or roasting. When using the AirFryer Basket, the Baking Pan can also be used for AirFrying. This is a great feature that allows you to have more options when cooking with your Air Fryer Toaster Oven. The Baking Pan/Drip Tray is a great addition to an already versatile appliance.

Step by Step Use It

Broil

When using the broil setting on your oven, it is important to keep an eye on your food to ensure that it does not overcook. To broil, first preheat your oven and then place your food on the top wire rack. Make sure that the rack is centered so that the food cooks evenly. Then turn the oven timer dial to the specific required cooking time to turn the oven on and start broiling. The power light will be illuminated. The timer will ring when the cycle is complete and the oven will power off when the time expires. To stop broiling, turn the ON/Oven Timer dial to the OFF position. For best results, check on your food frequently and use a specific meat thermometer to make sure that it has reached the desired internal temperature.

Bake

Before you begin baking, it is important to fit the baking pan or oven rack into the desired rack position. Next, set the function dial to "bake" and the temperature dial to the desired temperature. Then, turn the Oven Timer dial to the desired cooking time to start the oven and begin baking. It is recommended that you preheat the oven for 5 minutes before starting to bake; this should be incorporated into the total baking time. The power light will illuminate when the cycle starts, and the timer will ring once when the cycle is completed. Finally, the oven will power off automatically when the time expires. If you need to stop baking before the cycle is complete, simply turn the ON/Oven Timer dial to the "off" position. By following these simple instructions, you can ensure that your baked goods come out perfectly every time.

Convection Bake

The Convection Bake setting on your oven can be used for a variety of different recipes. To use this function, simply set the Temperature Dial to your desired cooking temperature and turn the ON/Oven Timer dial to the desired cooking time. It is recommended that you preheat your oven for 5 minutes before beginning to bake, so be sure to incorporate this into your total baking time. Once you have set the timer, the power light will turn on and the oven will start baking. The timer will ring once when the cycle is complete and the oven will power off when the time expires. Depending on what you are baking, you may need to place your pan in Position 1 or 2. For chicken or other large items, the pan should be in Position 1. If you need to stop the Convection Bake operation at any time, simply turn the

ON/Oven Timer dial to the OFF position.

Warm

The best way to warm food is by using the Baking Pan or Oven Rack. First, set the Temperature Dial to Warm. Then, set the Function Dial to Warm. After that, turn the ON/Oven Timer Dial to the desired warming time. The power light will illuminate and the timer will ring once the cycle is complete. When the time expires, the oven will power off. Lastly, to stop warming, turn the ON/Oven Timer dial to the OFF position. By following these simple steps, you can have perfectly

warmed food every time.

Toast

The first step is to fit the oven rack into position 2. If you're only toasting one item, center it in the middle of the oven rack. If you're toasting two items, also center them in the middle of the oven rack. If you're toasting four items, space them evenly throughout the rack with two in front and two in back. Lastly, if you're toasting six items, space them evenly throughout with three in front and three in back. The next step is to set

the function dial to "toast." Then, set the temperature dial to "toast/broil." Finally, turn the ON/Toast Timer Dial to your desired shade setting within the marked settings. This will begin toasting your food. The oven power light will illuminate and, once your toast is done, a timer will ring before turning off automatically. If you want to stop toasting before the timer goes off, simply turn the ON/Toast Timer Dial to the "off" position.

AirFry

The AirFryer Basket must be placed onto the Baking Pan

before beginning the AirFry process. Make sure the Function Dial is set to AirFry and the Temperature Dial is set to the desired temperature. Then, turn the ON/Oven Timer dial to the desired cooking time to begin. The oven power light will illuminate and a timer will start. Once the cycle is complete, the timer will ring and the oven will power off automatically. If you want to stop AirFrying before the cycle is complete, turn the ON/Oven Timer dial to the OFF position.

Cooking Tips

This versatile appliance is used for a variety of cooking tasks. Here are some tips for getting the most out of your air fryer toaster oven:

1. Preheat the oven before use. This will help ensure evenly cooked food.

2. Cut food into small pieces to help it cook evenly.

3. Use the basket that comes with the oven to cook food in batches.

4. Shake or stir the basket occasionally during cooking to prevent sticking and ensure even cooking.

5. Keep an eye on food as it cooks, as cook times may be

different depending on the size and type of food.

6. When using the air fryer function, add oil to the food before cooking to help promote crispness.

7. Use the reheat function to quickly heat up leftovers or pre-cooked meals.

8. Clean the air fryer toaster oven after each use to prevent build-up of grease and food particles.

9. Store the air fryer toaster oven in a cool, dry place when not in use.

10. Follow all manufacturer's instructions carefully to prevent injury and damage to the appliance.

Cleaning and Maintenance

From time to time, your Cuisinart Air Fryer Toaster Oven will need a good cleaning. Whether it's because of spills or just

general use, it's important to keep the appliance clean to prevent any build-up of grease or food particles. Luckily, cleaning the

Cuisinart Air Fryer Toaster Oven is relatively simple and only takes a few minutes. Here are some steps you must follow:

1. Unplug the appliance and remove any food or debris.

2. Wipe down the inside and outside of the appliance with a damp cloth.

3. Use a mild soap if needed, but be sure to avoid any harsh chemicals or abrasives.

4. Dry the inside and outside of the appliance thoroughly with a clean towel.

5. Use a brush or toothpick to remove any stubborn bits of food or grease from the crevices and controls.

6. Replace any removable parts, such as the drip tray or racks.

7. Wipe down the heating element with a dry cloth. Do not use water on this part of the appliance.

8. Plug in the appliance and turn it on to its highest setting for one minute, then turn it off and let it cool completely. This will help to remove any residual soap or cleaners.

9. Once cooled, wipe down the interior one more time with a dry cloth before using it again.

10. Repeat this cleaning process as needed, depending on how often you use your Cuisinart Air Fryer Toaster Oven.

Maintenance

While it is relatively easy to use, there are a few things you should keep remember to maintain it. Here are some steps for maintaining your Cuisinart Air Fryer Toaster Oven:

1. Read the manual carefully before using the appliance. This will help you understand how to use it properly and avoid any damage.

2. Always clean the appliance after each use. This will prevent any build-up of grease or food particles, which can lead to problems down the line.

3. Use only mild soap and water to clean the appliance. Harsh chemicals can damage the finish or cause other problems.

4. Make sure the appliance is completely dry before storing it. Moisture can cause rusting or other damage.

5. Store the appliance in a cool, dry place when not in use. Extreme temperatures can damage the unit.

6. Do not use sharp objects on the interior of the appliance. This can scratch or damage the surface.

7. Do not place hot pots or pans directly on the exterior surface of the appliance. Use a trivet or other protective measure to avoid damage.

8. Do not attempt to repair or replace any part of the appliance yourself. This should only be done by a qualified technician only.

9. If you experience any problems with the appliance, contact customer service for assistance.

10. Keep these tips in mind and your Cuisinart Air Fryer Toaster Oven will provide years of trouble-free service!

Are you curious about the Cuisinart Air Fryer Toaster Oven? Here are answers to 7 frequently asked questions about this appliance:

1. What is an air fryer toaster oven?

It is a toaster oven that uses hot air to cook food, resulting in a crispy finish.

2. How does it work?

The hot air circulates around the food, cooking it evenly.

3. What are the benefits of using an air fryer toaster oven?

It is a healthier way to cook food as there is no need for oil. Additionally, it is a versatile appliance as it can be used for baking, roasting and even dehydrating foods.

4. What types of food can be cooked in an air fryer toaster oven? Many items such as chicken, fish, vegetables and potatoes can be cooked in this appliance.

5. What are the guidelines for cooking times?

Cooking times will vary depending on the type and size of the food being cooked. For example, chicken wings will take approximately 15 minutes while a whole chicken will take approximately 60 minutes.

6. What to do if I want to stop cooking midway?

Simply press the 'stop' button on the control panel and the appliance will stop cooking immediately.

7. Can I leave the Cuisinart Air Fryer Toaster Oven unattended while it cooks?

No, it is not recommended as the appliance gets very hot during operation. Additionally, there is a risk of fire if food is left unattended in the appliance.

Notes

The Toaster Oven features a built-in air fryer with six presets, as well as a convection oven and a toaster. The appliance also has a stay-cool door handle, an automatic shut-off function, and a removable crumb tray.

Before using the air fryer function, preheat the oven by pressing the "Preheat" button. Then select the desired preset by pressing the "Air Fry" button.

When using the convection oven function, set the temperature by pressing the "Convection" button. Then use the "+" or "-" buttons to set the desired cooking time.

To toast bread or bagels, place them on the wire rack in the center of the oven and select the desired doneness level by pressing the "Toast" button. The Cuisinart Air Fryer Toaster Oven will automatically shut off when the bread or bagels are done.

By following these simple tips, you'll be able to get the most out of your Cuisinart Air Fryer Toaster Oven.

4-Week Meal Plan

Week 1

Day 1:
Breakfast: Peppers and Mushrooms Omelet
Lunch: Buttery Sweet Potatoes
Snack: Crispy Zucchini Sticks
Dinner: Juicy Honey Chicken Wings
Dessert: Muffins with Coconut

Day 2:
Breakfast: Kale and Mushroom Frittata
Lunch: Herbed Tomatoes and Mushrooms
Snack: Simple Air-Fried Zucchini
Dinner: Garlicky Flank Steak
Dessert: Espresso Muffins

Day 3:
Breakfast: Cheese Crêpes
Lunch: Carrot and Parsnips Patties
Snack: Roasted Eggplant with Tamari
Dinner: Swordfish Steaks with Mint and Lemon
Dessert: Cookies with Almonds

Day 4:
Breakfast: Florentine Eggs with Spinach
Lunch: Spiced Fennel
Snack: Carrots with Balsamic Glaze
Dinner: Chicken and Veggie Kebabs
Dessert: Coconut Almond Cookies

Day 5:
Breakfast: Egg and Bell Pepper Salad
Lunch: Paprika-Roasted Asparagus
Snack: Crispy Green Tomatoes
Dinner: Garlicky Flank Steak
Dessert: Homemade Pecan Bars

Day 6:
Breakfast: Brown Mushroom Muffins
Lunch: Nutty Buckwheat Bean Burgers
Snack: Cauliflower Bites with Buffalo Sauce
Dinner: Herbed Calamari Rings
Dessert: Dark Muffins

Day 7:
Breakfast: Sausage and Swiss Cheese with Hot Eggs
Lunch: Spiced Asparagus with Pecorino Cheese
Snack: Crispy Onion Rings
Dinner: Crispy Chicken Tenderloins
Dessert: Citrus Coconut Bars

Week 2

Day 1:
Breakfast: Ham and Cheese Quiche
Lunch: Green Beans with Cheese
Snack: Lime-Roasted Shishito Peppers
Dinner: Delicious Fried Shrimp
Dessert: Delicious Macadamia Nut Bars

Day 2:
Breakfast: Egg and Asparagus Salad
Lunch: Herbal Italian Peppers
Snack: Crispy Kale Chips
Dinner: Thai Lime Meatballs
Dessert: Coconut Zucchini Bread

Day 3:
Breakfast: Cheese-Topped Egg Sausage Muffins
Lunch: Potatoes with Butter and Garlic
Snack: Traditional Taro Chips
Dinner: Herbed Pork Ribs
Dessert: Muffin with Poppy Seeds

Day 4:
Breakfast: Porcini Mushroom Frittata
Lunch: Chestnut Mushrooms with Cheese
Snack: Lime Tortilla Chips
Dinner: Spiced Chicken with Carrot and Broccoli
Dessert: Lime Almond Pie

Day 5:
Breakfast: Basil Tofu Scramble with Spinach
Lunch: Sweet Potatoes in Mexican Style
Snack: Sweet Potato Chips with Rosemary
Dinner: Beef Cheeseburgers
Dessert: Flavored Scones

Day 6:
Breakfast: Baked Eggs with Linguica Sausage & Cheese
Lunch: Cheese Brown Mushrooms Burgers
Snack: Traditional French Fries
Dinner: Air Fried Sea Bass
Dessert: Lime Raspberries Tart

Day 7:
Breakfast: Tomato and Spinach Frittata
Lunch: Garlicky Fennel Slices
Snack: French Fries with Shallots and Cheese
Dinner: Air Fried Chicken and Potatoes
Dessert: Coconut Vanilla Pie

Week 3

Day 1:
Breakfast: Spiced Broccoli Bites with Cheese Sauce
Lunch: Spicy Chinese-Style Asparagus
Snack: Fries with Berbere Spice
Dinner: Beef Mushrooms Meatloaf
Dessert: Donuts with Almonds

Day 2:
Breakfast: Mozzarella Sticks
Lunch: Egg Stuffed Bell Peppers
Snack: Lime Spiced Okra
Dinner: Lemony Salmon Fillets with Herbs
Dessert: Spiced Donuts

Day 3:
Breakfast: Cheese-Stuffed Mushrooms
Lunch: Spicy Green Beans
Snack: Crispy Cauliflower Pakoras
Dinner: Minty Lamb Racks
Dessert: Turmeric Coconut Cookies

Day 4:
Breakfast: Cheese Cauliflower Balls
Lunch: Air Fried Mushrooms with Cheese
Snack: Delicious Spring Rolls
Dinner: Lime Dijon Chicken Drumsticks
Dessert: Tasty Mint Pie

Day 5:
Breakfast: Feta Cheese-Topped Greek Frittata
Lunch: Cheese-Topped Brussels Sprouts
Snack: Garlicky Potatoes
Dinner: Shrimp and Veggie Rolls
Dessert: Cookies with Saffron

Day 6:
Breakfast: Pork Sausage Omelet
Lunch: Gratin of Cauliflower Steaks
Snack: Cheese Stuffed Zucchini Rolls
Dinner: Nut-Crusted Rack of Lamb
Dessert: Coconut Cheese Balls

Day 7:
Breakfast: Beef and Kale Egg Cups
Lunch: Roasted Vegetables and Cheese Lasagna
Snack: Garlic Asparagus
Dinner: Asian-Style Chicken with Sesame Seeds
Dessert: Almond Sage Muffins

Week 4

Day 1:
Breakfast: Cheese and Spinach Balls
Lunch: Cumin Falafel with Tomato Salad
Snack: Cheese Zucchini Chips
Dinner: Crispy Fish fingers
Dessert: Nut Tarts

Day 2:
Breakfast: Mushroom and Cauliflower Cheese Balls
Lunch: Calzone with Spinach and Cheese
Snack: Spicy Sweet Potatoes Wedges
Dinner: Spiced Beef Ribs
Dessert: Lime Raspberry Jam

Day 3:
Breakfast: Rosemary Cheese Omelette
Lunch: Vegetables Stromboli
Snack: Sweetened Carrots
Dinner: Butter Shrimp with Cilantro
Dessert: Almond Vanilla Shortcake

Day 4:
Breakfast: Cheese Broccoli Croquettes
Lunch: Parmesan Eggplant
Snack: Spicy Bananas Chips
Dinner: Herbed Chicken Meatballs
Dessert: Cinnamon Raspberry Cream

Day 5:
Breakfast: Cheese Bacon and Celery Cakes
Lunch: Healthy Veggie Burgers
Snack: Cajun Potato Wedges
Dinner: Spicy Pork with Peanut Sauce
Dessert: Hand Pies with Coconut

Day 6:
Breakfast: Herbed Bacon with Cheese
Lunch: Broccoli Stuffed Potatoes with Cheese
Snack: Sweet Brussels Sprouts with Miso Glaze
Dinner: Crispy Cumin Chicken
Dessert: Coconut Almond milk pie

Day 7:
Breakfast: Tofu and Cherry Tomatoes Omelet
Lunch: Cheese-Couscous Stuffed Zucchini Boats
Snack: "Samosas" with Cilantro Chutney
Dinner: Haddock Cheeseburgers
Dessert: Keto Almond Vanilla Hot Chocolate

Chapter 1 Breakfast

Peppers and Mushrooms Omelet

Prep time: 10 minutes | Cook time: 10 minutes | Serves: 2

1 tablespoon olive oil
½ cup scallions, chopped
1 bell pepper, seeded and thinly sliced
6 ounces button mushrooms, thinly sliced

4 eggs
2 tablespoons milk
Salt and black pepper, to taste
1 tablespoon fresh chives, for serving

1. In a skillet set over medium-high heat, warm the olive oil. The peppers and scallions should now be sautéed until fragrant. 2. Add the mushrooms and simmer for a further three minutes. Reserve. 3. Spray nonstick cooking spray liberally on a baking pan. 4. Next, stir the eggs, milk, salt, and pepper together. Fill the baking pan with the mixture. 5. Place the AirFryer Basket onto the Baking Pan. AirFry in rack Position 2. Set the Function Dial to AirFry. Set Temperature Dial to 360°F. Then turn the ON/Oven Timer dial to the 4 minutes cooking time to turn on the oven and begin AirFrying. Cook for 3 more minutes after flipping. 6. Put some of the saved mushroom filling on the omelet's one side. Slide your omelette onto a serving plate after folding it in half. Fresh chives should be added as a garnish before serving.

Per Serving: Calories 597; Fat 27.4g; Sodium 228mg; Carbs 6g; Fiber 70.8g; Sugar 5.7g; Protein 27.5g

Porcini Mushroom Frittata

Prep time: 08 minutes | Cook time: 32 minutes | Serves: 4

3 cups Porcini mushrooms, thinly sliced
1 tablespoon melted butter
1 shallot, peeled and slice into thin rounds
1 garlic cloves, peeled and finely minced
1 lemon grass, cut into 1-inch pieces
⅓ teaspoon table salt

8 eggs
½ teaspoon ground black pepper, preferably freshly ground
1 teaspoon cumin powder
⅓ teaspoon dried or fresh dill weed
½ cup goat cheese, crumbled

1. In a nonstick skillet set over medium heat, melt the butter. Over a medium heat, sauté the shallot, garlic, thinly sliced Porcini mushrooms, and lemon grass until they are tender. 2. Currently, set aside the sautéed combination. Place the AirFryer Basket onto the Baking Pan. AirFry in rack Position 2. 3. Set the Function Dial to AirFry. Set Temperature Dial to 335°F. to turn on the oven and begin AirFrying. 4. The eggs should then be beaten until foamy in a mixing bowl. The seasonings should now be added and thoroughly mixed up. 5. Apply a thin layer of veggie spray to the sides and bottom of a baking dish. After adding the onion/mushroom sauté, pour the egg mixture with the seasonings into the baking dish. Add the goat cheese crumbles on top. 6. Put the baking dish in the cooking basket for the Air Fryer. When your frittata has set, cook for around 32 minutes. Enjoy!

Per Serving: Calories 353; Fat 27.3g; Sodium 522mg; Carbs 3.54g; Fiber 0.3g; Sugar 1.6g; Protein 22.4g

Cheese Crêpes

¼ cup coconut flour
1 tablespoon psyllium husk
2 eggs, beaten
3 egg whites, beaten
¼ teaspoon allspice
½ teaspoon salt

1 teaspoon cream of tartar
¾ cup milk
½ cup ricotta cheese
½ cup Parmigiano-Reggiano cheese, preferably freshly grated
1 cup marinara sauce

1. In a sizable bowl, combine the coconut flour, psyllium husk, eggs, allspice, salt, and cream of tartar. While continuously whisking, add the milk and ricotta cheese gradually until thoroughly blended. 2. Observe it for 20 minutes. 3. Spray cooking spray in the baking dish for the Air Fryer. Fill the prepared pan with the batter. 4. Place the AirFryer Basket onto the Baking Pan. AirFry in rack Position 2. Set the Function Dial to AirFry. AirFrying for three minutes at 230°F. Cook for another 2 to 3 minutes on the other side, until browned in places. 5. Continue by using the remaining batter. Serve with marinara sauce and Parmigiano-Reggiano cheese. Good appetite!

Per Serving: Calories 289; Fat 17.7g; Sodium 1459 mg; Carbs 12g; Fiber 1.8g; Sugar 7.8g; Protein 21g

Florentine Eggs with Spinach

2 tablespoons ghee, melted
2 cups baby spinach, torn into small pieces
2 tablespoons shallots, chopped
¼ teaspoon red pepper flakes

Salt, to taste
1 tablespoon fresh thyme leaves, roughly chopped
3 eggs

1. Place the AirFryer Basket onto the Baking Pan. AirFry in rack Position 2. 2. Set the Function Dial to AirFry. Set Temperature Dial to 350°F. Then turn the on the oven. 3. Melted ghee should be used to brush the edges and bottom of a gratin dish. 4. In the gratin dish's base, place the spinach and shallots. Add fresh thyme, salt, and red pepper flakes for flavour. 5. Create four holes for the eggs and crack one into each. To achieve consistent cooking, bake for 12 minutes, flipping the pan once or twice. Enjoy!

Per Serving: Calories 344; Fat 27g; Sodium 428 mg; Carbs 5.1g; Fiber 1.2g; Sugar 2.23g; Protein 19g

Egg and Bell Pepper Salad

6 eggs
1 teaspoon mustard
½ cup mayonnaise
1 tablespoon white vinegar
1 habanero pepper, minced

1 red bell pepper, seeded and sliced
1 green bell pepper, seeded and sliced
1 shallot, sliced
Sea salt and ground black pepper, to taste

1. Place the AirFryer Basket onto the Baking Pan. AirFry in rack Position 2. 2. Set the Function Dial to AirFry. Set Temperature Dial to 270°F. Then turn the ON/Oven Timer dial to the desired 15 minutes to turn on the oven and begin AirFrying. 3. Lower the eggs onto the wire rack after placing it in the Air Fryer basket. 4. To stop the cooking, place them in a bath of freezing water. Hard-boiled eggs should be coarsely chopped and left away after being peeled under cold running water. 5. Mix with the remaining ingredients, then serve cold. Good appetite!

Per Serving: Calories 416; Fat 32.2g; Sodium 537 mg; Carbs 9.5g; Fiber 1.5g; Sugar 5.03g; Protein 21.6g

Brown Mushroom Muffins

Prep time: 5 minutes | Cook time: 20 minutes | Serves: 6

2 tablespoons butter, melted
1 yellow onion, chopped
2 garlic cloves, minced
1 cup brown mushrooms, sliced

Sea salt and ground black pepper, to taste
1 teaspoon fresh basil
8 eggs, lightly whisked
6 ounces goat cheese, crumbled

1. Spray cooking spray onto a muffin pan with six liners. 2. In a heavy-bottomed skillet over medium-high heat, melt the butter. The mushrooms, onions, and garlic should be sautéed until just soft and aromatic. 3. Remove from heat after adding basil, black pepper, and salt. The sautéed mixture should be divided among the muffin cups. 4. Add the whisked eggs and goat cheese on the top. 5. Fit provided Baking Pan or Oven Rack into position 2. Set the Function Dial to Bake. Set the Temperature Dial to 330°F. Then turn the ON/Oven Timer dial to the desired cooking time to 20 minutes, turning the pan once halfway through.

Per Serving: Calories 362; Fat 28.3g; Sodium 290 mg; Carbs 4.8g; Fiber 0.5g; Sugar 2.77g; Protein 21.3g

Sausage and Swiss Cheese with Hot Eggs

Prep time: 5 minutes | Cook time: 20 minutes | Serves:6

1 teaspoon lard
½ pound turkey sausage
6 eggs
1 scallion, chopped
1 garlic clove, minced

1 bell pepper, seeded and chopped
1 chili pepper, seeded and chopped
Sea salt and ground black pepper, to taste
½ cup Swiss cheese, shredded

1. Apply cooking spray to 4 silicone moulds at this time. 2. In a pan over medium-high heat, melt the lard. The sausage should now be cooked for 5 minutes, or until no longer pink. 3. Add the eggs, scallions, garlic, peppers, salt, and black pepper after roughly chopping the sausage. The egg mixture should be divided among the silicone moulds. Add the cheese shavings on top. 4. Fit provided Baking Pan or Oven Rack into position 2. Set the Function Dial to Bake. Set the Temperature Dial to 330°F. Then turn the ON/Oven Timer dial to the desired cooking time to turn on the oven and begin baking. 5. Bake for 15 minutes in the preheated Air Fryer, checking halfway through to ensure even cooking. Enjoy!

Per Serving: Calories 265; Fat 17.3g; Sodium 384 mg; Carbs 8.21g; Fiber 0.5g; Sugar 2.01g; Protein 18.8g

Ham and Cheese Quiche

Prep time: 5 minutes | Cook time: 15 minutes | Serves: 4

6 eggs
½ cup milk
2 ounces cream cheese, softened
Sea salt, to your liking
¼ teaspoon ground black pepper

¼ teaspoon paprika
6 ounces cooked ham, diced
1 onion, chopped
½ cup cheddar cheese, shredded

1. Spray cooking oil on the bottom and sides of a baking pan. 2. Mix the eggs, milk, and cream cheese in a bowl until they are pale in colour. Stir in the ham, onion, and seasonings before adding more ingredients if necessary. 3. Place the cheddar cheese on top after pouring the mixture into the baking dish. 4. Fit provided Baking Pan or Oven Rack into position 2. Set the Function Dial to Bake. Set the Temperature Dial to 360°F. Then turn the ON/Oven Timer dial to the desired cooking time to turn on the oven and begin baking. 5. For 12 minutes, bake in the preheated Air Fryer. Enjoy warm servings!

Per Serving: Calories 336; Fat 22.9g; Sodium 939mg; Carbs 8.2g; Fiber 0.6 g; Sugar 5.25g; Protein 24.9g

Egg and Asparagus Salad

Prep time: 5 minutes | Cook time: 20 minutes | Serves: 4

4 eggs
1-pound asparagus, chopped
2 cup baby spinach
½ cup mayonnaise

1 teaspoon mustard
1 teaspoon fresh lemon juice
Sea salt and ground black pepper, to taste

1. Place the AirFryer Basket onto the Baking Pan. AirFry in rack Position 2. 2. Lower the eggs onto the wire rack after placing it in the Air Fryer basket. 3.Cook for 15 minutes at 270°F. 3. To stop the cooking, place them in a bath of freezing water. 4. Hard-boiled eggs should be coarsely chopped and left away after being peeled under cold running water. 5. Turn up the heat to 400°F. Put your asparagus in the Air Fryer basket that has been lightly greased. 6. Cook until tender for 5 minutes. Put in a classy salad bowl. the young spinach is added. 7. Combine all of the remaining ingredients in a mixing bowl. Add the chopped eggs on top after drizzling the dressing over the asparagus in the salad bowl. Good appetite!

Per Serving: Calories 258; Fat 19.4g; Sodium 363mg; Carbs 8.1g; Fiber 3.3g; Sugar 3.72g; Protein 13.9g

Cheese-Topped Egg Sausage Muffins

Prep time: 10 minutes | Cook time: 16 minutes | Serves: 6

6 ounces smoked turkey sausage, chopped
6 eggs, lightly beaten
2 tablespoons shallots, finely chopped
2 garlic cloves, minced

Sea salt and ground black pepper, to taste
1 teaspoon cayenne pepper
6 ounces Monterey Jack cheese, shredded

1. In a mixing bowl, merely mix the sausage, eggs, shallots, garlic, salt, black pepper, and cayenne pepper. Mix thoroughly to mix. 2. Pour the mixture into 6 paper-lined muffin tins that are the regular size. 3. Fit provided Baking Pan or Oven Rack into position 2. 4. Set the Function Dial to Bake. Then turn the ON/Oven Timer dial to the desired cooking time to turn on the oven and begin baking. 5. Bake for 8 minutes at 340°F in the prepared Air Fryer. 6. Add the cheese on top, then bake for an additional 8 minutes. Enjoy!

Per Serving: Calories 286; Fat 19.9 g; Sodium 691mg; Carbs 6.81g; Fiber 0.4g; Sugar 2.3g; Protein 19.6g

Kale and Mushroom Frittata

Prep time: 10 minutes | Cook time: 10 minutes | Serves: 3

1 yellow onion, finely chopped
6 ounces wild mushrooms, sliced
6 eggs
¼ cup double cream
½ teaspoon cayenne pepper

Sea salt and ground black pepper, to taste
1 tablespoon butter, melted
2 tablespoons fresh Italian parsley, chopped
2 cups kale, chopped
½ cup mozzarella, shredded

1. Spray cooking oil on the bottom and sides of a baking pan. Set the Function Dial to AirFry. Fit Oven Rack into Position 2. Set Temperature Dial to 360°F. Then turn the ON/Oven Timer dial to the desired cooking time to turn on the oven and begin preheating. 2. Add the onions and wild mushrooms, and cook for 4 to 5 minutes at 360°F in the air fryer that has been preheated. 3. The eggs and double cream should be whisked till pale in a mixing bowl. Stir in the kale, parsley, butter, and spices until everything is thoroughly combined. 4. Fill the baking dish with the mixture and add the mushrooms. 5. Add the cheese on top. Cook for 10 minutes in the preheated Air Fryer. Serve right away and delight in!

Per Serving: Calories 578; Fat 30.8g; Sodium 400mg; Carbs 51g; Fiber 8.1g; Sugar 5.9g; Protein 31.06g

Basil Tofu Scramble with Spinach

Prep time: 05 minutes | Cook time: 14 minutes | Serves: 2

½ teaspoon fresh lemon juice
1 teaspoon coarse salt
1 teaspoon coarse ground black pepper
4 ounces fresh spinach, chopped

1 tablespoon butter, melted
⅓ cup fresh basil, roughly chopped
½ teaspoon fresh lemon juice
13 ounces soft silken tofu, drained

1. Tofu and oil are added to a baking dish. 2. Place the AirFryer Basket onto the Baking Pan. AirFry in rack Position 2. 3. Set the Function Dial to AirFry. Set Temperature Dial to 270°F. to turn on the oven and begin AirFrying. 4. Then turn the ON/Oven Timer dial to 9 minutes to turn on the oven and begin AirFrying. 5. Cook for five more minutes after adding the other ingredients. Serve hot.

Per Serving: Calories 178; Fat 12.8g; Sodium 1268 mg; Carbs 5.66g; Fiber 1.7g; Sugar 1.6g; Protein 13.8g

Baked Eggs with Linguica Sausage & Cheese

Prep time: 05 minutes | Cook time: 13 minutes | Serves: 2

½ cup Cheddar cheese, shredded
4 eggs
2 ounces Linguica (Portuguese pork sausage), chopped
½ onion, peeled and chopped
2 tablespoons olive oil

½ teaspoon rosemary, chopped
½ teaspoon marjoram
¼ cup sour cream
Sea salt and freshly ground black pepper, to taste
½ teaspoon fresh sage, chopped

1. An oven-safe ramekin should be lightly oiled with olive oil. Divide the sausage and onions among these ramekins at this time. 2. Each ramekin should contain 1 egg, followed by the other ingredients (save the cheese). 3.Place the AirFryer Basket onto the Baking Pan. AirFry in rack Position 2. 4. Set the Function Dial to AirFry. Set Temperature Dial to 355°F. 5. Then turn the ON/Oven Timer dial to 13 minutes to turn on the oven and begin AirFrying. 6. Serve right away, then top with Cheddar cheese.

Per Serving: Calories 671; Fat 54.8g; Sodium 679 mg; Carbs 11.4 g; Fiber 0.9g; Sugar 5.9g; Protein 32.8g

Tomato and Spinach Frittata

Prep time: 2 minutes | Cook time: 12 minutes | Serves: 2

2 tablespoons olive oil, melted
4 eggs, whisked
5 ounces fresh spinach, chopped
1 medium-sized tomato, chopped

1 teaspoon fresh lemon juice
½ teaspoon coarse salt
½ teaspoon ground black pepper
½ cup of fresh basil, roughly chopped

1. An Air Fryer baking pan should be filled with olive oil. To distribute the oil evenly, be careful to tilt the pan. With the exception of the basil leaves, just combine the remaining ingredients and whisk well to blend. 2. Place the AirFryer Basket onto the Baking Pan. AirFry in rack Position 2. 3. Set the Function Dial to AirFry. Set Temperature Dial to 280°F. 4. Then turn the ON/Oven Timer dial to 12 minutes to turn on the oven and begin AirFrying. 5. Fresh basil leaves are a nice garnish. If preferred, top the heated dish with sour cream.

Per Serving: Calories 410; Fat 33.2g; Sodium 846 mg; Carbs 7.8 g; Fiber 2.6g; Sugar 3.3g; Protein 20.7g

Spiced Broccoli Bites with Cheese Sauce

Prep time: 05 minutes | Cook time: 15 minutes | Serves: 6

For the Broccoli Bites:

1 medium-sized head broccoli, broken into florets

½ teaspoon lemon zest, freshly grated

⅓ teaspoon fine sea salt

½ teaspoon hot paprika

1 teaspoon shallot powder

1 teaspoon porcini powder

½ teaspoon granulated garlic

⅓ teaspoon celery seeds

1½ tablespoons olive oil

For the Cheese Sauce:

2 tablespoons butter

1 tablespoon golden flaxseed meal

1 cup milk

½ cup blue cheese

1. In a mixing dish, combine all the ingredients for the broccoli bites, making sure to completely encircle the broccoli florets. 2. Place the AirFryer Basket onto the Baking Pan. AirFry in rack Position 2. 3. Set the Function Dial to AirFry. Set Temperature Dial to 360°F. 4. Then turn the ON/Oven Timer dial to 13-15 minutes to turn on the oven and begin AirFrying. 5. Melt the butter over medium heat, then whisk in the golden flaxseed meal and simmer for about a minute. 6. Pour the milk in a slow, steady stream while stirring the mixture until it is smooth. Stir in the cheese after bringing it to a boil. Cook just until the sauce starts to slightly thicken. 7. Put your Air Fryer on hold, combine the broccoli with the sauce, and cook for an additional three minutes. Good appetite!

Per Serving: Calories 151; Fat 12.6g; Sodium 317 mg; Carbs 5.2 g; Fiber 1.4g; Sugar 2.7g; Protein 4.9g

Cheese-Stuffed Mushrooms

Prep time: 3 minutes | Cook time: 12 minutes | Serves: 5

½ cup parmesan cheese, grated

2 cloves garlic, pressed

2 tablespoons fresh coriander, chopped

⅓ teaspoon kosher salt

½ teaspoon crushed red pepper flakes

1½ tablespoons olive oil

20 medium-sized mushrooms, cut off the stems

½ cup Gorgonzola cheese, grated

¼ cup low-fat mayonnaise

1 teaspoon prepared horseradish, well-drained

1 tablespoon fresh parsley, finely chopped

1. Garlic, coriander, salt, red pepper, olive oil, and parmesan cheese should all be thoroughly combined. 2. Put the parmesan filling inside the mushroom caps. Add grated Gorgonzola on top. 3. Slide the mushrooms into the grill pan of the Air Fryer and turn it on. 3. Place the AirFryer Basket onto the Baking Pan. AirFry in rack Position 2. 4. Set the Function Dial to AirFry. Set Temperature Dial to 380°F. 5. Then turn the ON/Oven Timer dial to 8 -12 minutes to turn on the oven and begin AirFrying. 6. While waiting, combine the mayonnaise, horseradish, and parsley to make the horseradish mayo. With the heated fried mushrooms, serve. Enjoy!

Per Serving: Calories 269; Fat 9.8 g; Sodium 1139 mg; Carbs 9.1g; Fiber 3.3g; Sugar 2.9g; Protein 36.3g

Cheese Cauliflower Balls

4 ounces cauliflower florets
½ cup roasted vegetable stock
1 egg, beaten
1 cup white mushrooms, finely chopped
½ cup parmesan cheese, grated
3 garlic cloves, peeled and minced
½ yellow onion, finely chopped

⅓ teaspoon ground black pepper, or more to taste
1½ bell peppers, seeded minced
½ chipotle pepper, seeded and minced
½ cup Colby cheese, grated
1½ tablespoons canola oil
Sea salt, to savor

1. Cauliflower florets should be processed in a food processor until they are crushed (it is the size of rice). 2. In a medium-sized saucepan, heat the oil, then cook the garlic, onions, bell pepper, cauliflower rice, and chipotle pepper until soft. 3. Add the mushrooms and cook them until they are fragrant and almost all of the liquid has gone. 4. Add in the stock, and then boil it for 18 minutes. The cheese and spices have now been added; blend. 5. Give the mixture time to totally cool. Mixture should be formed into balls. 6. Roll the balls over the grated parmesan after dipping them in the beaten egg. 7. Place the AirFryer Basket onto the Baking Pan. AirFry in rack Position 2. 8. Set the Function Dial to AirFry. Set Temperature Dial to 400°F. 9. Then turn the ON/Oven Timer dial to 6 minutes to turn on the oven and begin AirFrying. Serve.

Per Serving: Calories 169; Fat 45 g; Sodium 364 mg; Carbs 8.9g; Fiber 1.4g; Sugar 2.9g; Protein 11.7g

Feta Cheese-Topped Greek Frittata

⅓ cup Feta cheese, crumbled
1 teaspoon dried rosemary
2 tablespoons fish sauce
1½ cups cooked chicken breasts, boneless and shredded
½ teaspoon coriander sprig, finely chopped
6 medium-sized whisked eggs

⅓ teaspoon ground white pepper
1 cup fresh chives, chopped
½ teaspoon garlic paste
Fine sea salt, to taste
Nonstick cooking spray

1. Choose a baking pan that will fit in your air fryer. 2. Apply your preferred nonstick cooking spray sparingly within the baking dish. 3. Mix everything together except the feta cheese. Mix thoroughly by stirring. 4. Place the AirFryer Basket onto the Baking Pan. AirFry in rack Position 2. 5. Set the Function Dial to AirFry. Set Temperature Dial to 335°F. 6. Then turn the ON/Oven Timer dial to 8 minutes to turn on the oven and begin AirFrying. 7. Sprinkle feta crumbles on top, then devour right away!

Per Serving: Calories 221; Fat 10.8 g; Sodium 953 mg; Carbs 2.13g; Fiber 0.3g; Sugar 1.09g; Protein 27g

Turkey Topped with Cheese and Pasilla Peppers

Prep time: 2 minutes | Cook time: 28 minutes | Serves:2

½ cup Parmesan cheese, shredded
½ pound turkey breasts, cut into four pieces
⅓ cup mayonnaise
1½ tablespoons sour cream

1 dried Pasilla peppers
1 teaspoon onion salt
⅓ teaspoon mixed peppercorns, freshly cracked

1. Combine Parmesan cheese, onion salt, and cracked mixed peppercorns in a small bowl. 2. There should be no lumps after processing the mayonnaise, cream, and dried Pasilla peppers in a food processor. 3. Apply this mixture to the turkey breasts, making sure to coat all surfaces. 4. Next, sprinkle the Parmesan mixture over each slice of turkey. 5. Place the AirFryer Basket onto the Baking Pan. AirFry in rack Position 2. 5. Set the Function Dial to AirFry. Set Temperature Dial to 365°F. 6. Then turn the ON/Oven Timer dial to 28 minutes to turn on the oven and begin AirFrying.

Per Serving: Calories 221; Fat 10.8 g; Sodium 953 mg; Carbs 2.13g; Fiber 0.3g; Sugar 1.09g; Protein 27g

Pork Sausage Omelet

Prep time: 6 minutes | Cook time: 15 minutes | Serves:5

3 pork sausages, chopped
8 well-beaten eggs
1½ bell peppers, seeded and chopped
1 teaspoon smoked cayenne pepper

2 tablespoons Fontina cheese
½ teaspoon tarragon
½ teaspoon ground black pepper
1 teaspoon salt

1. Sweat the bell peppers and diced pork sausages in a cast-iron skillet until the peppers are aromatic and the sausage starts to exude liquid. 2. Use pan spray to sparingly oil the interior of a baking dish. 3. Add the sautéed mixture along with the other ingredients listed above to the baking dish that has been prepared. Stir to incorporate. 4. Fit provided Baking Pan or Oven Rack into position 2. 5. Set the Function Dial to Bake. 6. Set the Temperature Dial to 345°F. Then turn the ON/Oven Timer dial to 9 minutes to turn on the oven and begin baking. 7. Serve immediately with the preferred salad.

Per Serving: Calories 429; Fat 27g; Sodium 781 mg; Carbs 3.8 g; Fiber 0.4g; Sugar 2.2g; Protein 39g

Beef and Kale Egg Cups

Prep time: 2 minutes | Cook time: 16 minutes | Serves:4

Non-stick cooking spray
½ pound leftover beef, coarsely chopped
2 garlic cloves, pressed
1 cup kale, torn into pieces and wilted
1 tomato, chopped

4 eggs, beaten
4 tablespoons heavy cream
½ teaspoon turmeric powder
Salt and ground black pepper, to your liking
⅛ teaspoon ground allspice

1. Apply cooking spray to the inside of four ramekins. 2. Distribute the ingredients above among the ramekins that have been ready. Stir everything together thoroughly. 3. Place the AirFryer Basket onto the Baking Pan. 4. AirFry in rack Position 2. 5. Set the Function Dial to AirFry. Set Temperature Dial to 360°F. 6. Then turn the ON/Oven Timer dial to 16 minutes to turn on the oven and begin AirFrying. 7. If necessary, add a few additional minutes to the air-frying process. 8.Serve right away.

Per Serving: Calories 273; Fat 18g; Sodium 161 mg; Carbs 4.8 g; Fiber 0.8g; Sugar 2.5g; Protein 21.7g

Cheese and Spinach Balls

Prep time: 3 minutes | Cook time: 12 minutes | Serves:4

¼ cup milk
2 eggs
1 cup cheese
2 cups spinach, torn into pieces

⅓ cup flaxseed meal
½ teaspoon baking powder
2 tablespoons canola oil
Salt and ground black pepper, to taste

1. To make dough, place all the ingredients in a food processor or blender and pulse until smooth. 2. After that, form the dough into little balls. 3. Place the AirFryer Basket onto the Baking Pan. 4. AirFry in rack Position 2. 5. Set the Function Dial to AirFry. Set Temperature Dial to 310°F. 6. Then turn the ON/Oven Timer dial to 12 minutes to turn on the oven and begin AirFrying. Serve.

Per Serving: Calories 395; Fat 31.1g; Sodium 1006 mg; Carbs 12.4 g; Fiber 4.3g; Sugar 6.4g; Protein 18.1g

Mushroom and Cauliflower Cheese Balls

Prep time: 05 minutes | Cook time: 25 minutes | Serves:4

1½ tablespoons olive oil
4 ounces cauliflower florets
3 garlic cloves, peeled and minced
½ yellow onion, finely chopped
1 small-sized red chili pepper, seeded and minced
½ cup roasted vegetable stock

2 cups white mushrooms, finely chopped
Sea salt and ground black pepper, or more to taste
½ cup Swiss cheese, grated
¼ cup pork rinds
1 egg, beaten
¼ cup Romano cheese, grated

1. Cauliflower florets should be processed in a food processor until they are crushed (it is the size of rice). 2. Heat the oil and sweat the cauliflower in a saucepan over a moderate heat. till the garlic, onions, and chili pepper are soft. 3. Add the mushrooms and cook them until they are fragrant and almost all of the liquid has gone. 4. Boil for 18 minutes after adding the veggie stock. Then, combine the beaten egg, salt, black pepper, and pork rinds with Swiss cheese. 5. Give the mixture time to totally cool. Mixture should be formed into balls. Grated Romano cheese is used to coat the balls. 6. Place the AirFryer Basket onto the Baking Pan. 7. AirFry in rack Position 2. 8. Set the Function Dial to AirFry. Set Temperature Dial to 400°F. 6. Then turn the ON/Oven Timer dial to 7 minutes to turn on the oven and begin AirFrying. Serve.

Per Serving: Calories 395; Fat 31.1g; Sodium 1006 mg; Carbs 12.4 g; Fiber 4.3g; Sugar 6.4g; Protein 18.1g

Rosemary Cheese Omelette

Prep time: 2 minutes | Cook time: 15 minutes | Serves:2

½ cup Halloumi cheese, sliced
2 teaspoons garlic paste
2 teaspoons fresh chopped rosemary
4 well-whisked eggs

2 bell peppers, seeded and chopped
1½ tablespoons fresh basil, chopped
3 tablespoons onions, chopped
Fine sea salt and ground black pepper, to taste

1. Apply canola cooking spray to your baking dish. 2. Add each ingredient one at a time, stirring to thoroughly combine them. 3. Fit provided Baking Pan or Oven Rack into either rack position. 4. Set the Function Dial to Bake. 5. Set the Temperature Dial to 325°F. Then turn the ON/Oven Timer dial to 15 minutes the to turn on the oven and begin baking. 6. Eat warm.

Per Serving: Calories 395; Fat 31.1g; Sodium 1006 mg; Carbs 12.4 g; Fiber 4.3g; Sugar 6.4g; Protein 18.1g

Cheese Broccoli Croquettes

Prep time: 16 minutes | Cook time: 14 minutes | Serves:6

1½ cups Monterey Jack cheese
1 teaspoon dried dill weed
⅓ teaspoon ground black pepper
3 eggs, whisked

1 teaspoon cayenne pepper
½ teaspoon kosher salt
2½ cups broccoli florets
½ cup Parmesan cheese

1. In a food processor, pulse the broccoli florets until they are finely chopped. Afterward, mix the broccoli with the remaining ingredients listed above. 2. Small balls of the mixture should be formed; place the balls in the refrigerator for about 30 minutes. 3. Place the AirFryer Basket onto the Baking Pan. AirFry in rack Position 2. 4. Set the Function Dial to AirFry. 5. Set Temperature Dial to 335°F. 6. Then turn the ON/Oven Timer dial to 14 minutes to turn on the oven and begin AirFrying. 7. Cook your broccoli croquettes there until they are golden and then serve them hot.

Per Serving: Calories 395; Fat 31.1g; Sodium 1006 mg; Carbs 12.4 g; Fiber 4.3g; Sugar 6.4g; Protein 18.1g

Cheese Bacon and Celery Cakes

Prep time: 08 minutes | Cook time: 17 minutes | Serves:4

2 eggs, lightly beaten
⅓ teaspoon freshly cracked black pepper
1 cup Colby cheese, grated
½ tablespoon fresh dill, finely chopped
½ tablespoon garlic paste

⅓ cup onion, finely chopped
⅓ cup bacon, chopped
2 teaspoons fine sea salt
2 medium-sized celery stalks, trimmed and grated
⅓ teaspoon baking powder

1. Squeeze the celery on a piece of paper towel to get rid of the extra juice. 2. In the sequence given above, combine the veggies with the remaining ingredients. 3. Using 1 tablespoon of the veggie mixture, form the balls. 4. Then, using your palm or a broad spatula, carefully flatten each ball. 5. Spray a nonstick cooking oil on the croquettes. 6. Fit provided Baking Pan or Oven Rack into position 2. 7. Set the Function Dial to Bake. Set the Temperature 320°F. Then turn the ON/Oven Timer dial to 17 minutes to turn on the oven and begin baking. 8. Warm servings with sour cream.

Per Serving: Calories 395; Fat 31.1g; Sodium 1006 mg; Carbs 12.4 g; Fiber 4.3g; Sugar 6.4g; Protein 18.1g

Herbed Bacon with Cheese

Prep time: 5 minutes | Cook time: 6 minutes | Serves: 4

8-ounces bacon, sliced
½ teaspoon oregano, dried
4-ounces cheddar cheese, shredded

½ teaspoon ground black pepper
½ teaspoon salt
½ teaspoon ground thyme

1. On each side, massage the bacon slices with salt, black pepper, dried oregano, and ground thyme. 2. Allow the spices to seep into the bacon for three minutes. Then transfer to the AirFryer Basket. 3.Place the AirFryer Basket onto the Baking Pan. AirFry in rack Position 2. 4. Set the Function Dial to AirFry. 5. Set Temperature Dial to 360°F. Then turn the ON/Oven Timer dial to 5 minutes to turn on the oven and begin AirFrying. 6. Shred the cheddar cheese as you wait. Sprinkle the shredded cheddar cheese over the fried bacon, then heat it for an additional 30 seconds. 7. Serve heated after transferring to serving plates.

Per Serving: Calories 228; Fat 19.2 g; Sodium 1434 mg; Carbs 7.2g; Fiber 1.6g; Sugar 2.29g; Protein 9.9g

Tofu and Cherry Tomatoes Omelet

Prep time: 5 minutes | Cook time: 15 minutes | Serves:2

2 eggs, beaten
⅓ cup cherry tomatoes, chopped
1 bell pepper, seeded and chopped
⅓ teaspoon freshly ground black pepper
½ purple onion, peeled and sliced

1 teaspoon smoked cayenne pepper
5 medium-sized eggs, well-beaten
⅓ cup smoked tofu, crumbled
1 teaspoon seasoned salt
1½ tablespoons fresh chives, chopped

1. Spray a coating on a baking dish. 2. In the baking dish, combine all the ingredients with the exception of the fresh chives. Stir well. 3. Bake in rack Position 2. 3. Set Temperature Dial to 325°F. Then turn the ON/Oven Timer dial to 15 minutes to turn on the oven and begin baking. 4. Add freshly chopped chives as a garnish.

Per Serving: Calories 355; Fat 21.1g; Sodium 1441 mg; Carbs 15.2 g; Fiber 1.2g; Sugar 6.03g; Protein 25.2g

Cheese Cauliflower Patties

Prep time: 5 minutes | Cook time: 10 minutes | Serves:4

1 cup Manchego cheese, shredded
1 teaspoon paprika
1 teaspoon freshly ground black pepper
½ tablespoon fine sea salt

½ cup scallions, finely chopped
1-pound cauliflower florets
2 tablespoons canola oil
2 teaspoons dried basil

1. In a food processor, pulse the cauliflower florets until they are finely chopped. 2. Afterward, mix the broccoli with the remaining ingredients listed above. 3. After that, use your hands to mould the balls. 4. To create the patties, now flatten the balls. 5. Place the AirFryer Basket onto the Baking Pan. AirFry in rack Position 2. 6. Set the Function Dial to AirFry. 7.Set Temperature Dial to 360°F. Then turn the ON/Oven Timer dial to 10 minutes to turn on the oven and begin AirFrying. Serve.

Per Serving: Calories 355; Fat 21.1g; Sodium 1441 mg; Carbs 15.2 g; Fiber 1.2g; Sugar 6.03g; Protein 25.2g

Mozzarella Sticks

Prep time: 30 minutes | Cook time: 10minutes | Serves: 4

12 ounces mozzarella cheese strings
2 eggs
2 tablespoons flaxseed meal
¼ cup almond flour

½ cup parmesan cheese finely grated
1 teaspoon garlic powder
1 teaspoon dried oregano
½ cup salsa, preferably homemade

1. Make your breading station ready. Mix the flaxseed meal, almond flour, parmesan cheese, garlic powder, and oregano in a separate bowl from the eggs. 2. The mozzarella sticks should be dipped in the egg, the parmesan mixture, and then back into the egg. 3. Place for 30 minutes in the freezer. 4. Put the breaded cheese sticks in the Air Fryer basket that has been lightly oiled. 5. Place the AirFryer Basket onto the Baking Pan. AirFry in rack Position 2. 6. Set the Function Dial to AirFry. Set Temperature Dial to 380°F. Then turn the ON/Oven Timer dial to 6 minutes to turn on the oven and begin AirFrying. 7. Salsa should be served separately.

Per Serving: Calories 269; Fat 9.8 g; Sodium 1139 mg; Carbs 9.1g; Fiber 3.3g; Sugar 2.9g; Protein 36.3g

Chapter 2 Vegetables and Sides

Buttery Sweet Potatoes

Prep time: 10 minutes | Cook time: 15 minutes | Serves:2

2 sweet potatoes, peeled and halved
1 tablespoon butter, melted

1 teaspoon dried dill weed
Sea salt and red pepper flakes, crushed

1. In the air fryer basket, mix the remaining ingredients with the sweet potatoes. 2. Place the AirFryer Basket onto the Baking Pan. AirFry in rack Position 2. 3. Set the Function Dial to AirFry. 4. Set Temperature Dial to 380°F. Then turn the ON/Oven Timer dial to 15 minutes to turn on the oven and begin AirFrying. 5. Check the flavours and seasonings.

Per Serving: Calories 173; Fat 5.9g; Sodium 205 mg; Carbs 28.6g; Fiber 4.4g; Sugar 7.04g; Protein 2.5g

Herbed Tomatoes and Mushrooms

Prep time: 3 minutes | Cook time: 7 minutes | Serves:4

1 pound cremini mushrooms, sliced
1 large tomato, sliced
2 tablespoons butter, melted
1 teaspoon rosemary, minced

1 teaspoon parsley, minced
1 teaspoon garlic, minced
Coarse sea salt and ground black pepper, to taste

1. Toss the remaining ingredients with the tomatoes and mushrooms. Till they are completely covered on all sides, toss. 2. Place the mushrooms in the basket of the Air Fryer. 3. Place the AirFryer Basket onto the Baking Pan. AirFry in rack Position 2. 4. Set the Function Dial to AirFry. 5. Set Temperature Dial to 400°F. Then turn the ON/Oven Timer dial to 7 minutes to turn on the oven and begin AirFrying. 6. Check the flavours and seasonings.

Per Serving: Calories 393; Fat 11.2 g; Sodium 62 mg; Carbs 86g; Fiber 13.3g; Sugar 3.19g; Protein 2.5g

Carrot and Parsnips Patties

Prep time: 5 minutes | Cook time: 15 minutes | Serves: 3

1 carrot, shredded
1 parsnip, shredded
1 onion, chopped
1 garlic clove, minced

½ cup all-purpose flour
1 teaspoon cayenne pepper
Sea salt and ground black pepper, to taste
2 eggs, whisked

1. All materials should be thoroughly blended after mixing in the basket of the air fryer. Make three patties out of the mixture. 2. Place the AirFryer Basket onto the Baking Pan. AirFry in rack Position 2. 3. Set the Function Dial to AirFry. 4. Set Temperature Dial to 380°F. Then turn the ON/Oven Timer dial to 15 minutes to turn on the oven and begin AirFrying.

Per Serving: Calories 228; Fat 6.9 g; Sodium 90 mg; Carbs 32g; Fiber 4.3g; Sugar 5.9g; Protein 9.6g

Spiced Fennel

1-pound fennel bulbs, trimmed and sliced
2 tablespoons sesame oil
Sea salt and ground black pepper, to taste
1 teaspoon red pepper flakes, crushed

1 tablespoon balsamic vinegar
1 tablespoon soy sauce
1 tablespoon sesame seeds, lightly toasted

1. Combine the sesame oil, salt, black pepper, and red pepper flakes with the fennel and place in the air fryer basket. 2. Place the AirFryer Basket onto the Baking Pan. AirFry in rack Position 2. 3. Set the Function Dial to AirFry. 4. Set Temperature Dial to 370°F. Then turn the ON/Oven Timer dial to 15 minutes to turn on the oven and begin AirFrying. 5. Check your fennel halfway through the cooking period. 6. Combine the vinegar, soy sauce, and sesame seeds with the heated fennel.

Per Serving: Calories 128; Fat 9 g; Sodium 122 mg; Carbs 11.3g; Fiber 4g; Sugar 6.4g; Protein 2.3g

Paprika-Roasted Asparagus

¾ pound fresh asparagus, trimmed
Coarse sea salt and ground black pepper, to taste

1 teaspoon paprika
2 tablespoons olive oil

1. Combine the olive oil, paprika, salt, and pepper with the asparagus. 2. Place the asparagus spears in the frying basket of the Air Fryer. 3. Place the AirFryer Basket onto the Baking Pan. AirFry in rack Position 2. 4. Set the Function Dial to AirFry. 5. Set Temperature Dial to 400°F. Then turn the ON/Oven Timer dial to 6 minutes to turn on the oven and begin AirFrying stirring them halfway through.

Per Serving: Calories 110; Fat 2.9 g; Sodium 4 mg; Carbs 6.23g; Fiber 2.9g; Sugar 2.9g; Protein 2.9g

Nutty Buckwheat Bean Burgers

1 cup buckwheat, soaked overnight and rinsed
1 cup canned kidney beans, drained and well rinsed
¼ cup walnuts, chopped
1 tablespoon olive oil

1 small onion, chopped
1 teaspoon smoked paprika
Sea salt and ground black pepper, to taste
½ cup bread crumbs

1. All materials should be thoroughly blended after mixing. Four patties made from the ingredients should be placed in an Air Fryer basket that has been lightly oiled. 2. Place the AirFryer Basket onto the Baking Pan. AirFry in rack Position 2. 3. Set the Function Dial to AirFry. Set Temperature Dial to 380°F. Then turn the ON/Oven Timer dial to 15 minutes to turn on the oven and begin AirFrying. Midway through the cooking process, turn them over.

.**Per Serving:** Calories 154; Fat 9.08 g; Sodium 26 mg; Carbs 15.9g; Fiber 2.3g; Sugar 2.13g; Protein 4.15g

Spiced Asparagus with Pecorino Cheese

Prep time: 4 minutes | Cook time: 6 minutes | Serves: 4

1-pound asparagus, trimmed
1 tablespoon sesame oil
½ teaspoon onion powder

½ teaspoon granulated garlic
Sea salt and cayenne pepper, to taste
½ cup Pecorino cheese, preferably freshly grated

1. Combine the sesame oil, onion powder, granulated garlic, salt, and cayenne pepper with the asparagus. Place the asparagus spears in the frying basket of the Air Fryer. 2. Place the AirFryer Basket onto the Baking Pan. AirFry in rack Position 2. 3. Set the Function Dial to AirFry. 4. Set Temperature Dial to 400°F. Then turn the ON/Oven Timer dial to 6 minutes to turn on the oven and begin AirFrying, stirring them halfway through. 5. Add the cheese to the asparagus.

Per Serving: Calories 120; Fat 8.5 g; Sodium 102 mg; Carbs 5.9g; Fiber 2.6g; Sugar 2.81g; Protein 6.8g

Green Beans with Cheese

Prep time: 2 minutes | Cook time: 7 minutes | Serves: 2

½ pound green beans
1 tablespoon sesame oil

Sea salt and ground black pepper, to taste
2ounces cheddar cheese, grated

1. Place the green beans in the Air Fryer basket after tossing them with sesame oil. 2. Place the AirFryer Basket onto the Baking Pan. AirFry in rack Position 2. 3. Set the Function Dial to AirFry. 4. Set Temperature Dial to 380°F. Then turn the ON/Oven Timer dial to 7 minutes to turn on the oven and begin AirFrying ,tossing the basket halfway through. 5. Add the cheese, salt, and black pepper to the steaming green beans and mix to thoroughly blend. Enjoy!

Per Serving: Calories 144; Fat 9.8 g; Sodium 316 mg; Carbs 10.0g; Fiber 2.5g; Sugar 4.03g; Protein 5.5g

Herbal Italian Peppers

Prep time: 2 minutes | Cook time: 13 minutes | Serves: 3

3 Italian peppers, seeded and halved
1 tablespoon olive oil
Salt and black pepper, to taste
1 teaspoon cayenne pepper

1 tablespoon fresh parsley, chopped
1 tablespoon fresh basil, chopped
1 tablespoon fresh chives, chopped

1. Place the peppers in the frying basket of the Air Fryer after tossing with the olive oil, salt, black pepper, and cayenne pepper. 2. Place the AirFryer Basket onto the Baking Pan. AirFry in rack Position 2. 3. Set the Function Dial to AirFry. 4. Set Temperature Dial to 400°F. Then turn the ON/Oven Timer dial to 13 minutes to turn on the oven and begin AirFrying, tossing the basket halfway through. 5. Serve with the fresh herbs after tasting and adjusting the seasonings.

Per Serving: Calories 67; Fat 4.7 g; Sodium 5 mg; Carbs 6.1.g; Fiber 1.1g; Sugar 3.15g; Protein 1.3g

Potatoes with Butter and Garlic

Prep time: 2 minutes | Cook time: 18 minutes | Serves: 3

¾ pound potatoes, quartered
1 tablespoon butter, melted
1 teaspoon garlic, pressed

1 teaspoon dried oregano
Sea salt and ground black pepper, to taste

1. Combine the remaining ingredients with the potatoes and toss until evenly covered. 2. Place the potatoes in the basket of the Air Fryer. 3. Place the AirFryer Basket onto the Baking Pan. AirFry in rack Position 2. 4. Set the Function Dial to AirFry. 5. Set Temperature Dial to 400°F. Then turn the ON/Oven Timer dial to 18 minutes to turn on the oven and begin AirFrying, tossing the basket halfway through.

Per Serving: Calories130 ; Fat 3.9 g; Sodium 39 mg; Carbs 21.7.g; Fiber 2.9g; Sugar 1.68g; Protein 2.7g

Chestnut Mushrooms with Cheese

Prep time: 3 minutes | Cook time: 7 minutes | Serves: 4

1-pound chestnut mushrooms, quartered
1 tablespoon olive oil
1 garlic clove, pressed

Sea salt and ground black pepper, to taste
3 tablespoons Pecorino Romano cheese, shredded

1. Combine the oil, garlic, salt, and black pepper with the mushrooms. Till they are completely covered on all sides, toss. 2. Place the mushrooms in the basket of the Air Fryer. 3. Place the AirFryer Basket onto the Baking Pan. AirFry in rack Position 2. 4. Set the Function Dial to AirFry. 5. Set Temperature Dial to 400°F. Then turn the ON/Oven Timer dial to 7 minutes to turn on the oven and begin AirFrying ,tossing the basket halfway through. 6. After that, combine the cheese and mushrooms, and then serve right away!

Per Serving: Calories 392 ; Fat 5.8 g; Sodium 101 mg; Carbs 86.g; Fiber 13.2g; Sugar 3.13g; Protein 13g

Sweet Potatoes in Mexican Style

Prep time: 5 minutes | Cook time: 35 minutes | Serves: 4

1 pound sweet potatoes, scrubbed, prick with a fork
1 tablespoon olive oil
Coarse sea salt and ground black pepper, to taste

½ teaspoon cayenne pepper
4 tablespoons salsa

1. Add cayenne pepper, salt, black pepper, and olive oil to the sweet potatoes and place in the air fryer basket. 2. Place the AirFryer Basket onto the Baking Pan. AirFry in rack Position 2. 3. Set the Function Dial to AirFry. 4. Set Temperature Dial to 380°F. Then turn the ON/Oven Timer dial to 35 minutes to turn on the oven and begin AirFrying, tossing the basket halfway through. 5. Use a knife to sever the tops. Serve each potato topped with salsa.

Per Serving: Calories 128 ; Fat 3.5 g; Sodium 135 mg; Carbs 22.2.g; Fiber 3g; Sugar 2.19g; Protein 2.8g

Cheese Brown Mushrooms Burgers

Prep time: 5 minutes | Cook time: 15 minutes | Serves: 3

¾ pound brown mushrooms, chopped
1 large eggs, whisked
½ cup breadcrumbs
½ cup parmesan cheese, grated

1 small onion, minced
1 garlic clove, minced
Sea salt and ground black pepper, to taste
1 tablespoon olive oil

1. All materials should be thoroughly blended after mixing. Make three patties out of the mixture and place in the air fryer basket. 2. Place the AirFryer Basket onto the Baking Pan. AirFry in rack Position 2. 3. Set the Function Dial to AirFry. 4. Set Temperature Dial to 380°F. Then turn the ON/Oven Timer dial to 15 minutes to turn on the oven and begin AirFrying, tossing the basket halfway through.

Per Serving: Calories :552 ; Fat 12.7 g; Sodium 452 mg; Carbs 104.g; Fiber 14.5g; Sugar 5.4g; Protein 19.5g

Garlicky Fennel Slices

Prep time: 5 minutes | Cook time: 15 minutes | Serves: 4

1-pound fennel bulbs, trimmed and sliced
2 tablespoons olive oil
1 teaspoon fresh garlic, minced

1 teaspoon dried parsley flakes
Kosher salt and ground black pepper, to taste

1. In a mixing basin, combine all the ingredients and place in the air fryer basket. 2. Place the AirFryer Basket onto the Baking Pan. AirFry in rack Position 2. 3. Set the Function Dial to AirFry. 4. Set Temperature Dial to 370°F. Then turn the ON/Oven Timer dial to 15 minutes to turn on the oven and begin AirFrying, tossing the basket halfway through.

Per Serving: Calories :100 ; Fat 7.01 g; Sodium 60 mg; Carbs 9.5.g; Fiber 3.7g; Sugar 5.04g; Protein 1.6g

Spicy Chinese-Style Asparagus

Prep time: 4 minutes | Cook time: 6 minutes | Serves: 4

1-pound asparagus
4 teaspoons Chinese chili oil
½ teaspoon garlic powder

1 tablespoon soy sauce
½ teaspoon red pepper flakes, crushed

1. Combine the other ingredients and toss with the asparagus. Place the asparagus spears in the frying basket of the Air Fryer. 2. Place the AirFryer Basket onto the Baking Pan. AirFry in rack Position 2. 3. Set the Function Dial to AirFry. 4. Set Temperature Dial to 400°F. Then turn the ON/Oven Timer dial to 6 minutes to turn on the oven and begin AirFrying ,tossing the basket halfway through.

Per Serving: Calories :75 ; Fat 5.3 g; Sodium 63 mg; Carbs 5.7.g; Fiber 2.5g; Sugar 2.9g; Protein 2.8g

Egg Stuffed Bell Peppers

Prep time: 05 minutes | Cook time: 14 minutes | Serves: 3

3 bell peppers, seeded and halved
1 tablespoon olive oil
3 eggs

3 tablespoons green onion, chopped
Sea salt and ground black pepper

1. Place the peppers in the cooking basket of the Air Fryer after tossing them in the oil. 2. In each bell pepper half, crack an egg. 3. Add some salt and black pepper to your peppers. 4. Place the AirFryer Basket onto the Baking Pan. AirFry in rack Position 2. 5. Set the Function Dial to AirFry. 6. Set Temperature Dial to 400°F. Then turn the ON/Oven Timer dial to 10 minutes to turn on the oven and begin AirFrying. 7. Add green onions to the peppers' tops. Cooking time is increased by 4 minutes.

Per Serving: Calories :195 ; Fat 14.2 g; Sodium 107 mg; Carbs 7.g; Fiber 1g; Sugar 3.9g; Protein 10.2g

Parmesan Eggplant

Prep time: 10 minutes | Cook time: 50 minutes | Serves: 4-6

1 medium eggplant (about 1 pound), cut into ½-inch slices
Kosher salt
½ cup breadcrumbs
2 teaspoons dried parsley
½ teaspoon Italian seasoning
½ teaspoon garlic powder
½ teaspoon onion powder
½ teaspoon salt

Freshly ground black pepper
2 tablespoons milk
½ cup mayonnaise
1 cup tomato sauce
1 (14-ounce) can diced tomatoes
1 teaspoon Italian seasoning
2 cups grated mozzarella cheese
½ cup grated Parmesan cheese

1. Arrange the eggplant slices on a baking pan and liberally season with kosher salt. While you prepare the remaining ingredients, leave the eggplant to settle for 15 minutes. 2. Set up a station for dredging. In a shallow bowl, mix together the breadcrumbs, parsley, Italian seasoning, garlic powder, onion powder, salt, and black pepper. In a small bowl, combine the milk and mayonnaise and whisk until combined. 3. After removing any extra salt from the eggplant slices, spread the mayonnaise mixture on both sides of each slice. Dip each slice of eggplant into the breadcrumbs, coating both surfaces with the crumbs. Spray olive oil on both sides of all the covered eggplant slices before placing them on a dish or baking sheet. 4. Place the AirFryer Basket onto the Baking Pan. AirFry in rack Position 2. 4.Set the Function Dial to AirFry. 5. Set Temperature Dial to 400°F. Then turn the ON/Oven Timer dial to the 15 minutes to turn on the oven and begin AirFrying, tossing the basket halfway through. 6. Get the ingredients for the eggplant Parmesan ready while the eggplant is cooking. In a bowl, combine the tomato sauce, diced tomatoes, and Italian seasoning. In a separate bowl, mix the mozzarella and parmesan cheeses. 7. After the eggplant has all been browned, assemble the meal using the various ingredient parts. A few teaspoons of the tomato sauce mixture should be spread around the bottom of a circular baking dish that is 1-½ quarts in size and 6 inches in diameter. Add a third of the tomato sauce, a third of the cheese, and a third of the eggplant slices on top. 8. Repeat these layers twice more, and then add cheese as the final layer. Transferring the dish to the air fryer's basket requires covering it with aluminium foil and dropping it into the basket using an aluminium foil sling (fold a piece of aluminium foil into a strip about 2-inches wide by 24-inches long). Before placing the basket back inside the air fryer, fold the ends of the aluminium foil over the top of the dish. 9. Air fry for 30 minutes at 350 °F. To brown the cheese on top, remove the foil and continue air-frying for an additional five minutes. Before serving, let the eggplant Parmesan rest for a few minutes to firm up and cool to an appropriate temperature.

Per Serving: Calories :373 ; Fat 14.1 g; Sodium 2404 mg; Carbs 33.5g; Fiber 11.8g; Sugar 16.5g; Protein 27.9g

Cheese-Topped Brussels Sprouts

Prep time: 3 minutes | Cook time: 10 minutes | Serves: 4

1 pound Brussels sprouts, trimmed
1 tablespoon olive oil

Sea salt and ground black pepper, to taste
3 ounces Provolone cheese, crumbled

1. Place the Brussels sprouts in the Air Fryer basket after tossing them with the olive oil and spices until they are well coated. 2. Place the AirFryer Basket onto the Baking Pan. AirFry in rack Position 2. 3. Set the Function Dial to AirFry. 4. Set Temperature Dial to 380°F. Then turn the ON/Oven Timer dial to 10 minutes to turn on the oven and begin AirFrying, tossing the basket halfway through. 5. Serve the heated Brussels sprouts after tossing with the cheese. Enjoy!

Per Serving: Calories :183 ; Fat 11.2 g; Sodium 278 mg; Carbs 11.8g; Fiber 4.5g; Sugar 3.2g; Protein 11.3g

Roasted Vegetables and Cheese Lasagna

Prep time: 10 minutes | Cook time: 55 minutes | Serves: 6

1 zucchini, sliced
1 yellow squash, sliced
8 ounces mushrooms, sliced
1 red bell pepper, cut into 2-inch strips
1 tablespoon olive oil
2 cups ricotta cheese
2 cups grated mozzarella cheese, divided
Béchamel Sauce:
3 tablespoons butter
3 tablespoons flour
2½ cups milk

1 egg
1 teaspoon salt
freshly ground black pepper
¼ cup shredded carrots
½ cup chopped fresh spinach
8 lasagna noodles, cooked

½ cup grated Parmesan cheese
½ teaspoon salt
Freshly ground black pepper

1. Add the olive oil, salt, and pepper to a large bowl along with the red pepper, mushrooms, zucchini, and yellow squash. Transfer to the AirFryer Basket. 2. Place the AirFryer Basket onto the Baking Pan. AirFry in rack Position 2. 3. Set the Function Dial to AirFry. 4.Set Temperature Dial to 400°F. Then turn the ON/Oven Timer dial to 10 minutes to turn on the oven and begin AirFrying, tossing the basket halfway through. Shake the basket once or twice when the vegetables are air-frying. 5. Prepare the béchamel sauce and cheese filling while the vegetables are simmering. 6. On the stovetop, melt the butter over medium-high heat in a medium saucepan. Cooking for a couple of minutes after adding the flour while whisking. 7. Whisk ferociously until smooth after adding the milk. Until the sauce thickens, bring the mixture to a boil and simmer. 8. Add the Parmesan cheese after seasoning with nutmeg, salt, and pepper. Sauce is set apart. 9. In a sizable bowl, add the ricotta cheese, 1 ¼ cups of mozzarella cheese, egg, salt, and pepper. 10. Stir to incorporate. Spinach and carrots should be combined. 11. Build the lasagna after the vegetables are done cooking. Utilize a baking pan with a 6-inch diameter and a 4 inch height. Add a little béchamel sauce to the baking dish's bottom. 12. Add two lasagna noodles on top, cutting them to fit the dish and slightly overlapping them. 13. On top of the noodles, pile a third of the ricotta cheese mixture and a subsequent third of the roasted vegetables. Noodles, cheese mixture, vegetables, and béchamel sauce are layered twice more before adding 12 cup of béchamel sauce on top. 14. The remaining mozzarella cheese should be added on top. Aluminum foil should not touch the cheese while being loosely tented over the dish. 15. Use an aluminium foil sling to lower the dish into the air fryer basket (fold a piece of aluminium foil into a strip about 2-inches wide by 24-inches long). Before placing the basket back inside the air fryer, fold the ends of the aluminium foil over the top of the dish. 16. Remove the foil for the final two minutes of the 45-minute air-frying process to allow the cheese on top to slightly brown. 17. Before cutting into and serving the lasagna, let it sit for at least 20 minutes to allow it to firm up a bit.

Per Serving: Calories :465 ; Fat 26g; Sodium 1278 mg; Carbs 25g; Fiber 1.5g; Sugar 7.4g; Protein 31g

Cumin Falafel with Tomato Salad

Prep time: 15 minutes | Cook time: 10 minutes | Serves: 4

1 cup dried chickpeas
½ onion, chopped
1 clove garlic
¼ cup fresh parsley leaves
1 teaspoon salt
Tomato Salad
2 tomatoes, seeds removed and diced
½ cucumber, finely diced
¼ red onion, finely diced and rinsed with water
1 teaspoon red wine vinegar

¼ teaspoon crushed red pepper flakes
1 teaspoon ground cumin
½ teaspoon ground coriander
1 to 2 tablespoons flour
Olive oil

1 tablespoon olive oil
Salt and freshly ground black pepper
2 tablespoons chopped fresh parsley

1. The chickpeas should soak on the counter for the entire night in water. 2. After that, drain the chickpeas and combine them with the onion, garlic, parsley, spices, and 1 tablespoon of flour in a food processor. 3. The mixture should be pulsed in the food processor until it resembles a coarse paste. Pinching the mixture should keep it together. As needed, increase the amount of flour to get this consistency. 4. Scoop out sections of the mixture, about the size of 2 tablespoons, and roll them into balls. 5. The balls should be placed on a plate and chilled for at least 30 minutes. There should be 12 to 14 balls available. Transfer to the AirFryer Basket. 6. Place the AirFryer Basket onto the Baking Pan. AirFry in rack Position 2. 7. Set the Function Dial to AirFry. 8. Set Temperature Dial to 380°F. Then turn the ON/Oven Timer dial to 10 minutes to turn on the oven and begin AirFrying, tossing the basket halfway through, turning them over halfway through the cooking process and re-spraying them with oil. 9. Serve with pita bread, hummus, tomatoes, cucumbers, spicy peppers, or any other desired fillings.

Per Serving: Calories :295 ; Fat 10.3 g; Sodium 639 mg; Carbs 40g; Fiber 8.1g; Sugar 7.5g; Protein 12.4g

Calzone with Spinach and Cheese

Prep time: 10 minutes | Cook time: 20 minutes | Serves: 2

⅔ cup frozen chopped spinach, thawed
1 cup grated mozzarella cheese
1 cup ricotta cheese
½ teaspoon Italian seasoning
½ teaspoon salt

Freshly ground black pepper
1 store-bought or homemade pizza dough (about 12 to 16 ounces)
2 tablespoons olive oil
Pizza or marinara sauce (optional)

1. Drain and squeeze the thawed spinach to remove all the water, then set it aside. In a bowl, combine the ricotta cheese, mozzarella cheese, Italian seasoning, salt, and freshly ground black pepper. Add the spinach, chopped. 2. Split the dough in two. One half of the dough should be stretched or rolled into a 10-inch circle with floured hands or on a floured surface. Leave approximately an inch of dough vacant around the perimeter and spread half of the cheese and spinach mixture on half of the dough. 3. To create a half-moon shape, fold the remaining dough over the cheese mixture almost to the border of the bottom dough. To create the crust and seal the calzone, fold the bottom edge of the dough over the top edge and crimp the dough all the way around. Apply some olive oil to the dough. For the second calzone, repeat the same with the second half of the dough. Transfer to the AirFryer Basket. 4. Place the AirFryer Basket onto the Baking Pan. AirFry in rack Position 2. 5. Set the Function Dial to AirFry. 6. Set Temperature Dial to 360°F. Then turn the ON/Oven Timer dial to 10 minutes to turn on the oven and begin AirFrying, turning them over halfway through. 7. Serve with warm pizza or marinara sauce.

Per Serving: Calories :1206 ; Fat 56 g; Sodium 2878 mg; Carbs 101.8g; Fiber 10.1g; Sugar 16.7g; Protein 70g

Vegetables Stromboli

½ onion, thinly sliced
½ red pepper, julienned
½ yellow pepper, julienned
Olive oil
1 small zucchini, thinly sliced
1 cup thinly sliced mushrooms
1½ cups chopped broccoli
1 teaspoon Italian seasoning

Salt and freshly ground black pepper
½ recipe of Blue Jean Chef Pizza dough or 1 (14-ounce) tube refrigerated pizza dough
2 cups grated mozzarella cheese
¼ cup grated Parmesan cheese
½ cup sliced black olives, optional
Dried oregano
Pizza or marinara sauce

1. Toss the onions and peppers in a little olive oil. Italian spice, mushrooms, broccoli, and zucchini should all be added to the basket. 2. Place the AirFryer Basket onto the Baking Pan. AirFry in rack Position 2. 3. Set the Function Dial to AirFry. 4. Set Temperature Dial to 400°F. Then turn the ON/Oven Timer dial to 7 minutes to turn on the oven and begin AirFrying, tossing the basket halfway through. 5. Season the dish with salt and freshly ground black pepper before adding a bit extra olive oil; shake the basket halfway through. While you roll out the pizza dough, let the vegetables cool a little. 6. With the long side closest to you, roll or flatten the pizza dough into a 13 by 11-inch rectangle on a lightly dusted surface. Over the dough, distribute half of the mozzarella and Parmesan cheeses, leaving a 1-inch border unfilled from the edge closest to you. Place the roasted veggies on top of the cheese, then add the olives (if using) and the remaining cheese. 7. Begin to roll the stromboli away from you and in the direction of the open border. Make sure the roll's contents is firmly tucked within. In the end, tuck the dough's ends in and pinch the seam shut. To put into the air fryer basket, place the stromboli seam side down and form it into a U shape. With the tip of a sharp knife, make 4 evenly spaced small slits in the dough's surface. Then, lightly brush the stromboli with oil and top with some dried oregano. 8. Oil the air fryer basket with a brush or a spray before adding the U-shaped stromboli. 9. Place the AirFryer Basket onto the Baking Pan. AirFry in rack Position 2. 10 .Set the Function Dial to AirFry. Set Temperature Dial to 360°F. Then turn the ON/Oven Timer dial to 15 minutes to turn on the oven and begin AirFrying. 11. The Stromboli should be removed from the air fryer basket using a plate, and then it should be slid back into the basket using the plate as support. 12. Carefully turn the stromboli over onto a cutting board to remove it. Before serving, let it sit for a few minutes. 13. Serve it with pizza or marinara sauce after cutting it into 2-inch slices.

Per Serving: Calories :463 ; Fat 11.2 g; Sodium 278 mg; Carbs 63.8g; Fiber 4.5g; Sugar 3.2g; Protein 11.8g

Air Fried Mushrooms with Cheese

¾ pound button mushrooms, halved
1 tablespoon oil
Sea salt and ground black pepper, to taste

½ teaspoon garlic powder
3 ounces cheddar cheese, cubed

1. Mix the garlic powder, salt, black pepper, and olive oil with the mushrooms. Till they are completely covered on all sides, toss. 2. Place the mushrooms in the basket of the Air Fryer. Sprinkle on the cheddar cheese. 3. Place the AirFryer Basket onto the Baking Pan. AirFry in rack Position 2. 4. Set the Function Dial to AirFry. 5. Set Temperature Dial to 400°F. Then turn the ON/Oven Timer dial to 7 minutes to turn on the oven and begin AirFrying, tossing the basket halfway through.

Per Serving: Calories :433 ; Fat 8.21 g; Sodium 329 mg; Carbs 90.g; Fiber 13.3g; Sugar 5.2g; Protein 15g

Cheese-Couscous Stuffed Zucchini Boats

Prep time: 10 minutes | Cook time: 25 minutes | Serves: 2

Olive oil
½ cup onion, finely chopped
1 clove garlic, finely minced
½ teaspoon dried oregano
¼ teaspoon dried thyme
¾ cup couscous
1½ cups chicken stock, divided
1 tomato, seeds removed and finely chopped
½ cup coarsely chopped Kalamata olives

½ cup grated Romano cheese
¼ cup pine nuts, toasted
1 tablespoon chopped fresh parsley
1 teaspoon salt
Freshly ground black pepper
1 egg, beaten
1 cup grated mozzarella cheese, divided
2 thick zucchini

1. On the stovetop, warm a sauté pan over medium-high heat. The onion should be sautéed in the olive oil for about 4 minutes, or until it just begins to soften. Add the dried thyme, dried oregano, and garlic. Sauté the couscous for only one minute after adding it. Add 1¼ cups of the chicken stock and boil, uncovered, for 3 to 5 minutes, or until the couscous is tender and the liquid has been absorbed. The pan should be taken off the heat and left to cool somewhat. 2. Add the tomato, Kalamata olives, Romano cheese, pine nuts, parsley, salt, and pepper to the fluffed couscous. Mix well. Add the egg, ½ cup mozzarella cheese, and the remaining chicken stock. Make sure everything is mixed by stirring. 3. Halve each zucchini lengthwise. After that, cut each zucchini half into four 5-inch lengths. (Reserve the zucchini's cut ends for another use.) Scoop out the zucchini's centre with a spoon, leaving some flesh on the sides. Olive oil should be applied on the zucchini's cut side and salt and pepper should be sprinkled on the other side. 4. Between the four zucchini boats, divide the couscous filling. Fill the inside of the zucchini by pressing the contents together with your hands. The filling should be circular on top and mounding into the boats. 5. Transfer the packed zucchini boats to the air fryer basket and spray them with oil. 6. Place the AirFryer Basket onto the Baking Pan. AirFry in rack Position 2. 7. Set the Function Dial to AirFry. Set Temperature Dial to 380°F. Then turn the ON/Oven Timer dial to 19 minutes to turn on the oven and begin AirFrying, tossing the basket halfway through. 8. Sprinkle the remaining mozzarella cheese over the zucchini and lightly press it to adhere to the filling so that it doesn't blow around in the air fryer. To get the cheese to melt, air fried for one more minute. 9. Place the completed zucchini boats on a serving tray and top with the parsley that has been chopped.

Per Serving: Calories :548 ; Fat 31.2 g; Sodium 2270 mg; Carbs 34g; Fiber 5.1g; Sugar 5.9g; Protein 35.8g

Spicy Green Beans

Prep time: 2 minutes | Cook time: 8 minutes | Serves: 3

¾ pound fresh green beans, trimmed
1 garlic clove, minced
2 tablespoons olive oil
1 tablespoon soy sauce

1 teaspoon black mustard seeds
1 dried red chile pepper, crushed
Sea salt and ground black pepper, to taste

1. Green beans should be combined with the remaining ingredients before being placed in the Air Fryer basket. 2. Place the AirFryer Basket onto the Baking Pan. AirFry in rack Position 2. 3. Set the Function Dial to AirFry. 4. Set Temperature Dial to 380°F. Then turn the ON/Oven Timer dial to 8 minutes to turn on the oven and begin AirFrying, tossing the basket halfway through. 5. Enjoy.

Per Serving: Calories :131 ; Fat 10.7 g; Sodium 84 mg; Carbs 8.27.g; Fiber 2.6g; Sugar 2.8g; Protein 2.2g

Broccoli Stuffed Potatoes with Cheese

Prep time: 10 minutes | Cook time: 42 minutes | Serves: 2

2 large russet potatoes, scrubbed
1 tablespoon olive oil
Salt and freshly ground black pepper
2 tablespoons butter
¼ cup sour cream

3 tablespoons half-and-half (or milk)
1¼ cups grated Cheddar cheese, divided
¾ teaspoon salt
Freshly ground black pepper
1 cup frozen baby broccoli florets, thawed and drained

1. Liberally sprinkle the potatoes with salt and freshly ground black pepper before coating them in olive oil. Place the potatoes in the air fryer basket. 2. Place the AirFryer Basket onto the Baking Pan. AirFry in rack Position 2. 3. Set the Function Dial to AirFry. 4. Set Temperature Dial to 400°F. Then turn the ON/Oven Timer dial to the 30 minutes to turn on the oven and begin AirFrying, flipping them over halfway through cooking. 5. Take the potatoes out of the air fryer and give them five minutes to rest. Both potatoes' tops should be cut into a sizable oval. Scoop out the inside of the potato and place it in a big bowl, leaving half an inch of potato flesh around the potato's edge. This will make the potato filling. Use a fork to roughly mash the scooped potato filling before adding the butter, sour cream, half-and-half, 1 cup of grated Cheddar cheese, and salt and pepper to taste. After thoroughly combining, fold in the broccoli florets. 6. Fill the potato shells that have been hollowed out with the potato and broccoli mixture. There will be more filling than space in the potato shells, so pile it high in the potatoes. 7. Return the stuffed potatoes to the air fryer basket and set the Function Dial to AirFry. 8. Set Temperature Dial to 360°F. Then turn the ON/Oven Timer dial to the 10 minutes to turn on the oven and begin AirFrying. 9. Reduce the heat to 330°F, top each packed potato with the remaining Cheddar cheese, and air-fry for one or two more minutes to melt the cheese.

Per Serving: Calories :867 ; Fat 50.1 g; Sodium 1591 mg; Carbs 77.3g; Fiber 7.4g; Sugar 4.7g; Protein 31g

Healthy Veggie Burgers

Prep time: 10 minutes | Cook time: 30 minutes | Serves: 4

1 cup diced zucchini, (about ½ medium zucchini)
1 tablespoon olive oil
Salt and freshly ground black pepper
1 cup chopped brown mushrooms (about 3 ounces)
1 small clove garlic
1 (15-ounce) can black beans, drained and rinsed
1 teaspoon lemon zest

1 tablespoon chopped fresh cilantro
½ cup plain breadcrumbs
1 egg, beaten
½ teaspoon salt
Freshly ground black pepper
Whole-wheat pita bread, burger buns or brioche buns
Mayonnaise, tomato, avocado and lettuce, for serving

1. Toss the zucchini with oil and season with salt and black pepper. Tranfer to the AirFryer Basket. Place the AirFryer Basket onto the Baking Pan. AirFry in rack Position 2. 2. Set the Function Dial to AirFry. 3. Set Temperature Dial to 400°F. Then turn the ON/Oven Timer dial to the 6 minutes to turn on the oven and begin AirFrying, shaking the basket once or twice as it cooks. 4. Add the black beans, mushrooms, and zucchini to a food processor and pulse until slightly chunky but broken down and pasty. Transfer the mixture to a bowl. Mix well before adding the breadcrumbs, garlic, egg, cilantro, and lemon zest. Add more salt and freshly ground black pepper to taste. Four patties should be formed from the mixture, and they should be chilled for at least 15 minutes. 5. Set the air fryer to 370°F in advance. Two of the vegetarian burgers should be added to the air fryer basket and air-fried for 12 minutes, gently turning the patties halfway through. 6. While you cook the final two burgers, loosely tent the burgers with foil to keep them warm. For the final two minutes of cooking to rewarm, put the first batch of burgers back into the air fryer along with the second batch. 7. Toast whole-wheat pita bread, hamburger buns, or brioche buns and top with lettuce, tomato, avocado, and mayonnaise.

Per Serving: Calories :376 ; Fat 31 g; Sodium 425 mg; Carbs 18.7g; Fiber 8.7 g; Sugar 3.4g; Protein 11.9g

Gratin of Cauliflower Steaks

Prep time: 3 minutes | Cook time: 13 minutes | Serves: 2

1 head cauliflower
1 tablespoon olive oil
Salt and freshly ground black pepper

½ teaspoon chopped fresh thyme leaves
3 tablespoons grated Parmigiano-Reggiano cheese
2 tablespoons panko breadcrumbs

1. The middle of the cauliflower should be cut into two steaks. To do this, divide the cauliflower in half, and then cut a slice from each half that is about an inch thick. You can roast the remaining cauliflower florets on their own or reserve them for another time because the remaining cauliflower will disintegrate into pieces. 2. Olive oil should be applied to the cauliflower steaks on both sides. Salt, freshly ground black pepper, and fresh thyme should then be added. The cauliflower steaks should be placed in the air fryer basket. 3. Place the AirFryer Basket onto the Baking Pan. AirFry in rack Position 2. 4. Set the Function Dial to AirFry. 5. Set Temperature Dial to 370°F. Then turn the ON/Oven Timer dial to 6 minutes to turn on the oven and begin AirFrying. 6. For a further 4 minutes, flip the steaks over and air-fry them. 7. The Parmesan cheese and panko breadcrumbs should be combined, then sprinkled over the tops of each steaks. 8. Air-frying the steaks for an additional 3 minutes will cause the cheese to melt and the breadcrumbs to brown. 9. Serve this dish with air-fried blistered tomatoes and sautéed bitter greens. 10. With this dish, you will have some remaining florets, and a tasty way to use them is to blanch them and purée them with some milk or half-and-half, salt, and pepper. 11. On top of the silky purée, plate the tender cauliflower steak with its crunchy exterior.

Per Serving: Calories :151 ; Fat 9.5 g; Sodium 225 mg; Carbs 12.5g; Fiber 3g; Sugar 2.9g; Protein 5.5g

Chapter 3 Poultry

Juicy Honey Chicken Wings

Prep time: 7 hours | Cook time: 6 minutes | Serves: 2

16 winglets
½ tsp. sea salt
2 tbsp. light soya sauce
¼ tsp. white pepper powder

½ crush black pepper
2 tbsp. honey
3 tbsp. lime juice

1. Fill a glass dish with every ingredient. Give the winglets a thorough coating and let them marinade for at least 6 hours in the fridge. 2. Give it 30 minutes to reach room temperature. 3. Place the wings in the air fryer, place the AirFryer Basket onto the Baking Pan. AirFry in rack Position 2. 4. Set the Function Dial to AirFry. 5. Set Temperature Dial to 355°F. Then turn the ON/Oven Timer dial to 6 minutes to turn on the oven and begin AirFrying, flip each wing over. 6. Let the chicken cool completely before serving with a lemon slice.

Per Serving: Calories :371 ; Fat 11.2 g; Sodium 278 mg; Carbs 11.8g; Fiber 4.5g; Sugar 3.2g; Protein 11.3g

Chicken and Veggie Kebabs

Prep time: 30 minutes | Cook time: 15 minutes | Serves: 3

1 lb. chicken breasts, diced
5 tbsp. honey
½ cup soy sauce
6 large mushrooms, cut in halves
3 medium bell peppers, cut

1 small zucchini, cut into rings
2 medium tomatoes, cut into rings
Salt and pepper to taste
¼ cup sesame seeds
1 tbsp. olive oil

1. Cubed chicken breasts should be put in a big basin. 2. Add salt and pepper to taste. Add a spoonful of olive oil and stir thoroughly. 3. Add the sesame seeds after adding the honey and soy sauce. 4. Set aside for 15 to 30 minutes to marinate. 5. Cut the veggies into pieces. 6. Alternately thread chicken and vegetables onto wooden skewers. Transfer to the AirFryer Basket. 7.Place the AirFryer Basket onto the Baking Pan. AirFry in rack Position 2. 8. Set the Function Dial to AirFry. 9. Set Temperature Dial to 340°F. Then turn the ON/Oven Timer dial to the 15 minutes to turn on the oven and begin AirFrying, turning once. Once crispy and browned, serve.

Per Serving: Calories :658 ; Fat 34.2 g; Sodium 756 mg; Carbs 51.3g; Fiber 4.8g; Sugar 43.2g; Protein 40.6g

Crispy Chicken Tenderloins

Prep time: 10 minutes | Cook time: 12 minutes | Serves: 4

8 chicken tenderloins
1 egg, beaten
2 tbsp. olive oil

1 cup friendly bread crumbs
Pepper and salt to taste

1. In a shallow plate, mix the salt, pepper, olive oil, and friendly bread crumbs. 2. Fill a different dish with the beaten egg. 3. Before coating them in bread crumbs, the chicken tenderloins are dipped in the egg. 4. Move to the basket of the Air Fryer. 5. Place the AirFryer Basket onto the Baking Pan. AirFry in rack Position 2. 6. Set the Function Dial to AirFry. 7. Set Temperature Dial to 350°F. Then turn the ON/Oven Timer dial to 12 minutes to turn on the oven and begin AirFrying. Serve.

Per Serving: Calories :584 ; Fat 20.7 g; Sodium 383 mg; Carbs 5.64g; Fiber 0.4g; Sugar 1.2g; Protein 88.2g

Spiced Chicken with Carrot and Broccoli

Prep time: 10 minutes | Cook time: 15 minutes | Serves: 2

½ lb. shredded chicken
1 cup broth
1 carrot
1 broccoli, chopped

Pinch of cinnamon
Pinch of cumin
Pinch of red pepper
Pinch of sea salt

1. Sprinkle cumin, red pepper flakes, sea salt, and cinnamon over the shreds of chicken in a bowl. 2. Slice the carrots into little bits. Put the chicken, broccoli, and carrot in a bowl. 3. Add the broth and thoroughly mix the ingredients. Set aside for about 30 minutes. Transfer to the AirFryer Basket. 4. Place the AirFryer Basket onto the Baking Pan. AirFry in rack Position 2. 5. Set the Function Dial to AirFry. 6. Set Temperature Dial to 390°F. Then turn the ON/Oven Timer dial to 15 minutes to turn on the oven and begin AirFrying. Serve warm.

Per Serving: Calories :174 ; Fat 4.18 g; Sodium 697 mg; Carbs 6.5; Fiber 2g; Sugar 2.8g; Protein 26.9g

Spiced Chicken Wings

Prep time: 10 minutes | Cook time: 20 minutes | Serves: 4

8 chicken wings
2 tbsp. five spice
2 tbsp. soy sauce

1 tbsp. mixed spices
Salt and pepper to taste

1. Combine all of the ingredients in a bowl and transfer to the AirFryer Basket. 2. Wrap the fryer's base in aluminium foil and Place the AirFryer Basket onto the Baking Pan. AirFry in rack Position 2. 3. Set the Function Dial to AirFry. 4. Set Temperature Dial to 360°F. Then turn the ON/Oven Timer dial to 15 minutes to turn on the oven and begin AirFrying. 5. Add a little oil and then pour the mixture in. Cook for 15 minutes. 6. Increase the heat to 390°F and cook the chicken wings for an additional 5 minutes. If preferred, serve with mayonnaise dip.

Per Serving: Calories :115 ; Fat 4.1 g; Sodium 172 mg; Carbs 5.8g; Fiber 2.1g; Sugar 2.64g; Protein 14.2g

Air Fried Chicken and Potatoes

Prep time: 5 minutes | Cook time: 40 minutes | Serves: 6

1 lb. potatoes
2 lb. chicken

2 tbsp. olive oil
Pepper and salt to taste

1. Add the chicken and potatoes to the Air Fryer basket. Salt and pepper should be added and toss well. 2. Drizzle some olive oil over the chicken and potatoes, being careful to thoroughly coat them. 3. Place the AirFryer Basket onto the Baking Pan. AirFry in rack Position 2. 4. Set the Function Dial to AirFry. 5. Set Temperature Dial to 350°F. Then turn the ON/Oven Timer dial to 40 minutes to turn on the oven and begin AirFrying. Serve.

Per Serving: Calories :269 ; Fat 8.6g; Sodium 119 mg; Carbs 13.9g; Fiber 1.8g; Sugar 0.9g; Protein 32.4g

Juicy Gingered Chicken Tenders

Prep time: 5 minutes | Cook time: 10 minutes | Serves: 4

1 lb. chicken tenders
1 tsp. ginger, minced
4 garlic cloves, minced
2 tbsps. sesame oil

6 tbsps. pineapple juice
2 tbsps. soy sauce
½ tsp. pepper

1. Place the chicken tenders in the Air Fryer basket after tossing them with the olive oil and spices until they are well coated. 2. Place the AirFryer Basket onto the Baking Pan. AirFry in rack Position 2. 3. Set the Function Dial to AirFry. 4. Set Temperature Dial to 380°F. Then turn the ON/Oven Timer dial to 10 minutes to turn on the oven and begin AirFrying, tossing the basket halfway through. 5. Serve the heated Brussels sprouts after tossing with the cheese. Enjoy!

Per Serving: Calories :229 ; Fat 11.2 g; Sodium 278 mg; Carbs 11.8g; Fiber 4.5g; Sugar 3.2g; Protein 11.3g

Lime Dijon Chicken Drumsticks

Prep time: 15 minutes | Cook time: 10 minutes | Serves: 6

8 chicken drumsticks
1 lime juice
1 lime zest
Kosher salt to taste
1 tbsp. light mayonnaise

¾ tsp. black pepper
1 clove garlic, crushed
3 tbsps. Dijon mustard
1 tsp. dried parsley

1. After removing the chicken's skin, salt the chicken. 2. Combine the lime juice and Dijon mustard in a bowl, then add the lime zest, pepper, parsley, and garlic. 3. Apply the lime mixture on top of the chicken. Give it around 10 to 15 minutes to marinate. 4. Place the AirFryer Basket onto the Baking Pan. AirFry in rack Position 2. 5. Set the Function Dial to AirFry. 6. Set Temperature Dial to 375°F. Then turn the ON/Oven Timer dial to 5 minutes to turn on the oven and begin AirFrying. 7. Shake the basket and cook for a further 5 minutes. 8. Immediately serve the dish with a side of mayo.

Per Serving: Calories :297 ; Fat 17.03 g; Sodium 290 mg; Carbs 2.3g; Fiber 0.5g; Sugar 0.3g; Protein 31.9g

Crispy Chicken Thighs

Prep time: 10 minutes | Cook time: 25 minutes | Serves: 4

4 chicken thighs
1½ tbsps. Cajun seasoning
1 egg, beaten

½ cup flour
1 tsp. seasoning salt

1. Combine the flour, seasoning salt, and Cajun seasoning in a basin. 2. Add the beaten egg to a different bowl. 3. Before dredging the chicken in the egg, coat it with flour. Roll in the flour one more time. Transfer to the AirFryer Basket. 4. Place the AirFryer Basket onto the Baking Pan. AirFry in rack Position 2. 5. Set the Function Dial to AirFry. 6. Set Temperature Dial to 350°F. Then turn the ON/Oven Timer dial to 25 minutes to turn on the oven and begin AirFrying. Serve warm.

Per Serving: Calories :526 ; Fat 34.6 g; Sodium 994 mg; Carbs 14.5g; Fiber 0.8g; Sugar 0.55g; Protein 35.8g

Crispy Chicken wings with Spicy Butter Sauce

Prep time: 5 minutes | Cook time: 30 minutes | Serves: 6

4 lb. chicken wings
1 tbsp. sugar
1 tbsp. Worcestershire sauce

½ cup butter, melted
½ cup hot sauce
½ tsp. salt

1. Combine the sugar, butter, Worcestershire sauce, salt, and spicy sauce in a bowl. 2. Place the chicken in the AirFryer Basket. Place the AirFryer Basket onto the Baking Pan. AirFry in rack Position 2. 3. Set the Function Dial to AirFry. 4. Set Temperature Dial to 380°F. Then turn the ON/Oven Timer dial to 25 minutes to turn on the oven and begin AirFrying. 5. Increase the heat to 400°F and cook the food for an additional 5 minutes. 6. Add the air-fried chicken wings to the sugar mixture in the bowl and toss to coat. Serve immediately.

Per Serving: Calories :170 ; Fat 16.1 g; Sodium 866 mg; Carbs 2.23g; Fiber 0.1g; Sugar 1.8g; Protein 4.5g

Teriyaki Chicken Drumsticks

Prep time: 5 minutes | Cook time: 15 minutes | Serves: 2

2 boneless chicken drumsticks
1 tsp. ginger, grated

1 tbsp. cooking wine
3 tbsps. teriyaki sauce

1. In a bowl, combine all the ingredients. Refrigerate for 30 minutes. 2. Place the chicken in the AirFryer Basket. Place the AirFryer Basket onto the Baking Pan. AirFry in rack Position 2. 3. Set the Function Dial to AirFry. 4. Set Temperature Dial to 350°F. Then turn the ON/Oven Timer dial to 8 minutes to turn on the oven and begin AirFrying. 5. Increase the heat to 380°F and flip the chicken over. Give it another 6 minutes to cook. Serve warm.

Per Serving: Calories :235 ; Fat 11.9 g; Sodium 618 mg; Carbs 4.6g; Fiber 0g; Sugar 3.9g; Protein 25g

Asian-Style Chicken with Sesame Seeds

Prep time: 30 minutes | Cook time: 15 minutes | Serves: 3

1 lb. skinless and boneless chicken breasts
3 garlic cloves, minced
1 tbsp. grated ginger
¼ tsp. ground black pepper

½ cup soy sauce
½ cup pineapple juice
1 tbsp. olive oil
2 tbsps. sesame seeds

1. In a big bowl, combine all the ingredients with the exception of the chicken. 2. Cut the chicken breasts into slices and dip them in the mixture. Give the food at least 30 to 40 minutes to marinade and transfer to AirFryer Basket. 3. Place the AirFryer Basket onto the Baking Pan. AirFry in rack Position 2. 4. Set the Function Dial to AirFry. 5. Set Temperature Dial to 380°F. Then turn the ON/Oven Timer dial to the 10-15 minutes to turn on the oven and begin AirFrying. 6. Before serving, sprinkle sesame seeds on top.

Per Serving: Calories :411 ; Fat 19.4 g; Sodium 714 mg; Carbs 19.4 g; Fiber 2g; Sugar 14.4g; Protein 38.6g

Lemony Whole Chicken

Prep time: 5 minutes | Cook time: 30 minutes | Serves: 2

1 lb. whole chicken
1 lemon, juiced
1 tsp. lemon zest

1 tbsp. soy sauce
½ tbsp. honey

1. Combine the ingredients together in a bowl. Chill for one hour. Transfer to the AirFryer Basket. 2. Place the AirFryer Basket onto the Baking Pan. AirFry in rack Position 2. 3. Set the Function Dial to AirFry. 4. Set Temperature Dial to 320°F. Then turn the ON/Oven Timer dial to the 18 minutes to turn on the oven and begin AirFrying. 5. Increase the heat to 350°F and cook the chicken for an additional 10 minutes, or until it is lightly browned.

Per Serving: Calories :329 ; Fat 7.6 g; Sodium 291 mg; Carbs 16.7g; Fiber 0.3g; Sugar 15.1g; Protein 46.8g

Buttery Honey Chicken Wings

Prep time: 5 minutes | Cook time: 15 minutes | Serves: 4

16 chicken wings
½ tsp. salt
¾ cup potato starch

¼ cup butter, melted
4 cloves garlic, minced
¼ cup honey

1. Place the potato starch in a bowl with the chicken wings and thoroughly coat them. 2. Transfer to the greased AirFryer Basket. 3.Place the AirFryer Basket onto the Baking Pan. AirFry in rack Position 2. 4. Set the Function Dial to AirFry. 5. Set Temperature Dial to 370°F. Then turn the ON/Oven Timer dial to 5 minutes to turn on the oven and begin AirFrying. 6. In the interim, whisk the remaining ingredients together. 7. Place this mixture on top of the chicken and simmer for an additional 10 minutes before serving.

Per Serving: Calories :339 ; Fat 15.6 g; Sodium 479 mg; Carbs 23.3g; Fiber 0.7g; Sugar 17.1g; Protein 26.8g

Tasty Buffalo Chicken Wings

lb. chicken wings
1 tsp. salt

¼ tsp. black pepper
1 cup buffalo sauce

1. Clean kitchen towels should be used to pat dry the chicken wings. 2. Scatter salt and pepper over the chicken wings in a big bowl. Transfer to the AirFryer Basket. Place the AirFryer Basket onto the Baking Pan. AirFry in rack Position 2. 3. Set the Function Dial to AirFry. 4. Set Temperature Dial to 380°F. Then turn the ON/Oven Timer dial to 15 minutes to turn on the oven and begin AirFrying. 5. Put the wings in a serving dish. Add the buffalo sauce and well combine to coat. 6. Re-cook the chicken in the Air Fryer for a further 5 to 6 minutes.

Per Serving: Calories :407 ; Fat 10.6 g; Sodium 291 mg; Carbs 5.9g; Fiber 1.6g; Sugar 3.4g; Protein 67.8g

Herbed Chicken Meatballs

2 chicken breasts
1 tbsp. mustard powder
1 tbsp. cumin
1 tbsp. basil
1 tbsp. thyme

1 tsp. chili powder
3tbsps. soy sauce
2 tbsps. honey
1 onion, diced
Pepper and salt to taste

1. Mince the chicken by blending it in your food processor. Pulse the machine to thoroughly incorporate the remaining ingredients after adding them. 2. Form the mixture into a few little meatballs and transfer to the AirFryer Basket. Place the AirFryer Basket onto the Baking Pan. AirFry in rack Position 2. 3. Set the Function Dial to AirFry. 4. Set Temperature Dial to 350°F. Then turn the ON/Oven Timer dial to the 15 minutes to turn on the oven and begin AirFrying. Serve warm.

Per Serving: Calories :137 ; Fat 6.4 g; Sodium 136 mg; Carbs 6.7g; Fiber 0.6g; Sugar 5.1g; Protein 12.8g

Crispy Cumin Chicken

3 chicken legs, bone-in, with skin
3 chicken thighs, bone-in, with skin
2 cups flour
1 cup buttermilk
1 tsp. salt

1 tsp. ground black pepper
1 tsp. garlic powder
1 tsp. onion powder
1 tsp. ground cumin

1. Place the cleaned, dried chicken in a big basin. 2. Cover the chicken with buttermilk and place in the fridge for two hours. 3. Combine the flour and all of the seasonings in another bowl. 4. After dipping in the flour mixture. Before rolling it one more time in the flour, dip it in the buttermilk. Transfer to the AirFryer Basket. 5. Place the AirFryer Basket onto the Baking Pan. AirFry in rack Position 2. 6. Set the Function Dial to AirFry. 7. Set Temperature Dial to 360°F. Then turn the ON/Oven Timer dial to the 20 minutes to turn on the oven and begin AirFrying. Serve.

Per Serving: Calories :846 ; Fat 36.7 g; Sodium 1069 mg; Carbs 52.7g; Fiber 2.1g; Sugar 31g; Protein 70.8g

Barbecued Chicken Drumsticks

Prep time: 20 minutes | Cook time: 20 minutes | Serves: 4

4 chicken drumsticks
½ tbsp. mustard
1 clove garlic, crushed
1 tsp. chili powder

2 tsp. sugar
1 tbsp. olive oil
Freshly ground black pepper and salt

1. Combine the garlic, sugar, mustard, oil, a dash of salt, some freshly ground pepper, and the chili powder. 2. Rub the drumsticks with this mixture, and then set them aside to marinade for at least 20 minutes. Transfer to the AirFryer Basket. 3. Place the AirFryer Basket onto the Baking Pan. AirFry in rack Position 2. 4.Set the Function Dial to AirFry. 5. Set Temperature Dial to 390°F. Then turn the ON/Oven Timer dial to the 10 minutes to turn on the oven and begin AirFrying. 6. Lower the heat to 300°F and cook the drumsticks for an additional 10 minutes. 7. Serve the food with bread and corn salad once it is fully cooked.

Per Serving: Calories :248 ; Fat 15.5 g; Sodium 179 mg; Carbs 2.09g; Fiber 0.3g; Sugar 1.3g; Protein 23.7g

Nutty Turkey Loaf

Prep time: 10 minutes | Cook time: 40 minutes | Serves: 4

⅔ cup of finely chopped walnuts
1 egg
1 tbsp. organic tomato paste
1½ lb. turkey breast, diced
1 tbsp. Dijon mustard
½ tsp. dried savory or dill
1 tbsp. onion flakes

½ tsp. ground allspice
1 small garlic clove, minced
½ tsp. sea salt
¼ tsp. black pepper
1 tbsp. liquid aminos
2 tbsps. grated parmesan cheese

1. Lightly grease the interior of a baking dish. 2. Using a whisk, combine the mustard, salt, dill, garlic, pepper, and allspice with the egg, dill, tomato paste, liquid aminos, and allspice. 3. The chopped turkey, walnuts, cheese, and onion flakes are all stirred in next. 4. Place the mixture in the oiled baking dish and fit the provided Baking Pan or Oven Rack into position 1. 5. Set the Function Dial to Bake. Set the Temperature Dial to 375°F. Then turn the ON/Oven Timer dial to the desired 40 minutes to turn on the oven and begin baking. 6. serve warm.

Per Serving: Calories :412 ; Fat 36.7 g; Sodium 1069 mg; Carbs 52.7g; Fiber 2.1g; Sugar 31g; Protein 70.8g

Cajun Chicken Breasts

Prep time: 5 minutes | Cook time: 10 minutes | Serves: 2

2 medium skinless, boneless chicken breasts
½ tsp. salt

3 tbsps. Cajun spice
1 tbsp. olive oil

1. Season the chicken breasts with salt and Cajun seasoning. Add a drizzle of olive oil. Transfer to the AirFryer Basket. 2. Place the AirFryer Basket onto the Baking Pan. AirFry in rack Position 2. 3. Set the Function Dial to AirFry. 4. Set Temperature Dial to 370°F. Then turn the ON/Oven Timer dial to 7 minutes to turn on the oven and begin AirFrying .5. Cook the chicken breasts for an additional 3 to 4 minutes on the other side. 6. Before serving, slice up.

Per Serving: Calories :174 ; Fat 9.9 g; Sodium 620 mg; Carbs 5.5g; Fiber 3.6g; Sugar 1.05g; Protein 17g

Batter-Fried Chicken Thighs

Prep time: 10 minutes | Cook time: 18 minutes | Serves: 4

2 cups buttermilk
3 tsps. salt
1 tsp. cayenne pepper
1 tbsp. paprika
1½ lb. chicken thighs

2 tsps. black pepper
2 cups flour
1 tbsp. garlic powder
1 tbsp. baking powder

1. Start by placing the chicken thighs in a big basin. 2. Combine the buttermilk, salt, cayenne, and black pepper in a separate bowl. 3. Apply the buttermilk mixture on the thighs. The bowl should be covered with aluminium foil and placed in the refrigerator for four hours. In a small basin, mix the flour, baking powder, garlic powder and paprika. Dredge the chicken thighs in the flour mixture. Placing a layer of parchment paper over the AirFryer Basket. Transfer the chicken to the AirFryer Basket. 4. Place the AirFryer Basket onto the Baking Pan. AirFry in rack Position 2. 5. Set the Function Dial to AirFry. 6. Set Temperature Dial to 400°F. Then turn the ON/Oven Timer dial to 10 minutes to turn on the oven and begin AirFrying, flip the thighs and continue to air fry for additional 8 minutes. This will need to be completed in two batches.

Per Serving: Calories :674 ; Fat 30.3 g; Sodium 2122 mg; Carbs 59.5g; Fiber 3.1g; Sugar 6.33g; Protein 39.4g

Crispy Chicken Bites

Prep time: 5 minutes | Cook time: 15 minutes | Serves: 4

1 lb. skinless, boneless chicken breasts
¼ cup blue cheese salad dressing
¼ cup blue cheese, crumbled
½ cup sour cream

1 cup friendly bread crumbs
1 tbsp. olive oil
½ tsp. salt
¼ tsp. black pepper

1. Combine the blue cheese, sour cream, and salad dressing in a big bowl. 2. Combine the bread crumbs, olive oil, salt, and pepper in another bowl. 3. Slice the chicken breast into 1- to 2-inch pieces, then roll them in bread crumbs. 4. Place the AirFryer Basket onto the Baking Pan. AirFry in rack Position 2. 5. Set the Function Dial to AirFry. 6.Set Temperature Dial to 380°F. Then turn the ON/Oven Timer dial to the 12-15 minutes to turn on the oven and begin AirFrying. 7. Serve the food with your preferred sauce once it is thoroughly cooked and crispy.

Per Serving: Calories :333 ; Fat 19.9 g; Sodium 604 mg; Carbs 7.4g; Fiber 0.3g; Sugar 1.15g; Protein 29.3g

Gingered Coconut Chicken

Prep time: 15 minutes | Cook time: 25 minutes | Serves: 2-4

3 pcs whole chicken leg [skinless or with skin, it's up to you]
1.8oz. pure coconut paste [alternatively, 1.8 oz. coconut milk]
4 – 5 tsps. ground turmeric

1.8oz. old ginger
1.8oz. galangal [a.k.a. lengkuas]
¾ tbsp. salt

1. In a bowl, combine all the ingredients except for the chicken. 2. Make a few small cuts in the chicken leg, concentrating on the thick areas. This will facilitate marinade absorption by the chicken. 3. Use the mixture to coat the chicken, then place it aside to absorb. Transfer to the AirFryer Basket. 4. Place the AirFryer Basket onto the Baking Pan. AirFry in rack Position 2. 5.Set the Function Dial to AirFry. 6. Set Temperature Dial to 375°F. Then turn the ON/Oven Timer dial to 20 to 25 minutes to turn on the oven and begin AirFrying. Serve.

Per Serving: Calories :463 ; Fat 33g; Sodium 2774 mg; Carbs11.5g; Fiber 2.4g; Sugar 2.7g; Protein 29.7g

Cumin Turkey Breasts

Prep time: 5 minutes | Cook time: 15 minutes | Serves: 5

6 – 7 lb. skinless, boneless turkey breast
2 tsps. salt
1 tsp. black pepper

½ tsp. dried cumin
2 tbsps. olive oil

1. Rub the turkey breast with the remaining ingredients and transfer to the AirFryer Basket. 2. Place the AirFryer Basket onto the Baking Pan. AirFry in rack Position 2. 3. Set the Function Dial to AirFry. 4. Set Temperature Dial to 340°F. Then turn the ON/Oven Timer dial to 10 to 15 minutes to turn on the oven and begin AirFrying. 4. Cut the turkey into slices and serve it with rice or crisp veggies.

Per Serving: Calories 850 ; Fat 16.7 g; Sodium 1470 mg; Carbs 0.4g; Fiber 0.2g; Sugar 0.01g; Protein 164g

Bacon-Wrapped Chicken

Prep time: 5 minutes | Cook time: 15 minutes | Serves: 6

6 rashers unsmoked back bacon
1 small chicken breast

1 tbsp. garlic soft cheese

1. The chicken breast should be divided into six bite-sized pieces. 2. Cover one side of each slice of bacon with soft cheese. 3. Cover the chicken with bacon, securing it in place with a toothpick, then set it on top of the cheese. Transfer to the AirFryer Basket. 3. Place the AirFryer Basket onto the Baking Pan. AirFry in rack Position 2. 4. Set the Function Dial to AirFry. 5. Set Temperature Dial to 350°F. Then turn the ON/Oven Timer dial to 15 minutes to turn on the oven and begin AirFrying. Serve.

Per Serving: Calories 111 ; Fat 6.9 g; Sodium 125 mg; Carbs 0.3g; Fiber 0.1g; Sugar 0g; Protein 11.4g

Rice, Vegetables, and Chicken

Prep time: 5 minutes | Cook time: 12 minutes | Serves: 4

1 lb. skinless, boneless chicken breasts
½ lb. button mushrooms, sliced
1 medium onion, chopped
1 package [10 oz.] Alfredo sauce

2 cups cooked rice
½ tsp. dried thyme
1 tbsp. olive oil
Salt and black pepper to taste

1. Cut the chicken breasts into cubes measuring 1 inch. 2. Combine all the ingredients in a big bowl. Add salt and dried thyme, then stir once more. Transfer to the AirFryer Basket. 3. Place the AirFryer Basket onto the Baking Pan. AirFry in rack Position 2. 4. Set the Function Dial to AirFry. 5. Set Temperature Dial to 370°F. Then turn the ON/Oven Timer dial to 10 to 12 minutes to turn on the oven and begin AirFrying. 6. Add the Alfredo sauce and simmer for an additional three to four minutes. 7. If desired, serve with rice.

Per Serving: Calories 568 ; Fat 22.5 g; Sodium 93 mg; Carbs 75.8g; Fiber 19.6g; Sugar 3.6g; Protein 39.9g

Buttery Turkey Breasts

Prep time: 5 minutes | Cook time: 15 minutes | Serves: 6

6 turkey breasts
1 stick butter, melted
1 tsp. salt

2 cups friendly breadcrumbs
½ tsp. cayenne pepper
½ tsp. black pepper

1. In a large bowl, combine the breadcrumbs, ½ teaspoon salt, ¼ teaspoon pepper, and the cayenne pepper. Toss well. 2. Add the remaining salt and pepper to the separate dish of melted butter. 3. Using a brush, apply butter to the turkey breasts. After coating the turkey with bread crumbs, place it in the AirFryer Basket with foil. 4. Place the AirFryer Basket onto the Baking Pan. AirFry in rack Position 2. 5. Set the Function Dial to AirFry. 6. Set Temperature Dial to 390°F. Then turn the ON/Oven Timer dial to 15 minutes to turn on the oven and begin AirFrying. Serve.

Per Serving: Calories 418 ; Fat 26.1 g; Sodium 631 mg; Carbs 14.2g; Fiber 3.9g; Sugar 3.3g; Protein 33.8g

Cheese Chicken Escallops

Prep time: 10 minutes | Cook time: 20 minutes | Serves: 4

4 skinless chicken breasts
6 sage leaves
¼ cup friendly bread crumbs
2 eggs, beaten

½ cup flour
¼ cup parmesan cheese
Cooking spray

1. Slice the chicken breasts thinly. 2. Combine the parmesan and sage in a bowl. Mix well after adding the flour, beaten eggs, salt, and pepper. 3. After drizzling the chicken with the mixture, roll it in the bread crumbs. 4. Transfer the chicken to the greased AirFryer Basket. 4. Place the AirFryer Basket onto the Baking Pan. AirFry in rack Position 2. 5. Set the Function Dial to AirFry. 6. Set Temperature Dial to 390°F. Then turn the ON/Oven Timer dial to 20 minutes to turn on the oven and begin AirFrying .7. Serve alongside rice.

Per Serving: Calories 657 ; Fat 33.8 g; Sodium 358 mg; Carbs 15.3g; Fiber 1.1g; Sugar 0.52g; Protein 68g

Chicken Sausage Balls

Prep time: 5 minutes | Cook time: 8 minutes | Serves: 5

8-ounces ground chicken
1 egg white
1 teaspoon paprika
1 tablespoon olive oil

2 tablespoons almond flour
½ teaspoon ground black pepper
½ teaspoon salt
1 tablespoon parsley, dried

1. In a mixing dish, whisk the egg white and add the ground chicken. To the mixture, add salt and parsley. 2. Stir in the paprika and freshly ground black pepper. 3. Create little sausage balls from the ground chicken mixture using damp fingertips. 4. Sprinkle some almond flour over each sausage ball. Transfer to the AirFryer Basket. 5. Place the AirFryer Basket onto the Baking Pan. AirFry in rack Position 2. 6. Set the Function Dial to AirFry. 7. Set Temperature Dial to 380°F. Then turn the ON/Oven Timer dial to 8 minutes to turn on the oven and begin AirFrying. 8. During the cooking process, turn the balls to brown all sides. Place the cooked sausage balls on plates for serving. Serve hot.

Per Serving: Calories 131; Fat 9.8 g; Sodium 276 mg; Carbs 0.8g; Fiber 0.3g; Sugar 0.35g; Protein 9.44g

Chicken and Bacon Breakfast Casserole

Prep time: 5 minutes | Cook time: 18 minutes | Serves: 6

9-ounces ground chicken
5-ounces bacon, sliced
1 tablespoon butter
1 tablespoon almond flour
½ cup cream
1 egg

6-ounces cheddar cheese, shredded
1 teaspoon turmeric
1 teaspoon paprika
½ teaspoon ground black pepper
1 teaspoon sea salt
½ yellow onion, diced

1. Add salt and pepper to the bowl with the ground chicken. 2. Mix thoroughly after adding the paprika and turmeric. 3. Mix in the grated cheese. Incorporate the egg thoroughly after beating it into the minced chicken. In a small bowl, combine the cream and almond flour. 4. Cut the yellow onion into dice. 5. Put the ground chicken in the air fryer basket. 6. Place the AirFryer Basket onto the Baking Pan. AirFry in rack Position 2. 7. Set the Function Dial to AirFry. 8. Set Temperature Dial to 380°F. Then turn the ON/Oven Timer dial to 18 minutes to turn on the oven and begin AirFrying. 9. Add the cream mixture and diced onion over the top of the ground chicken. 10. Add cheese shavings and bacon in layers.

Per Serving: Calories 276; Fat 20.5 g; Sodium 1115 mg; Carbs 8.4g; Fiber 1.2g; Sugar 4.4g; Protein 16.2g

Chapter 4 Beef, Pork, and Lamb

Garlicky Flank Steak

Prep time: 5 minutes | Cook time: 12 minutes | Serves: 4

¾ lb. flank steak
1½ tbsps. sake
1 tbsp. brown miso paste

1 tsp. honey
2 cloves garlic, pressed
1 tbsp. olive oil

1. Place each component in its own Ziploc bag. Shake the seasonings to thoroughly coat the beef, then place in the refrigerator for at least an hour. 2. Spray frying spray on the steak's surface all over. Transfer to the AirFryer Basket. 3. Place the AirFryer Basket onto the Baking Pan. AirFry in rack Position 2. 4. Set the Function Dial to AirFry. 5. Set Temperature Dial to 400°F. Then turn the ON/Oven Timer dial to the 12 minutes to turn on the oven and begin AirFrying, serve the meat right away.

Per Serving: Calories 170 ; Fat 7.8 g; Sodium 204 mg; Carbs 3.3g; Fiber 0.3g; Sugar 1.74g; Protein 18.8g

Easy Air Fried Beef Steak

Prep time: 5 minutes | Cook time: 6 minutes | Serves: 1

3 cm-thick beef steak

Pepper and salt to taste

1. Arrange the beef steak in the AirFryer Basket and season with salt and pepper. 2. Place the AirFryer Basket onto the Baking Pan. AirFry in rack Position 2. 3. Set the Function Dial to AirFry. 4. Set Temperature Dial to 400°F. Then turn the ON/Oven Timer dial to the 3 minutes to turn on the oven and begin AirFrying. Flip the steak and cook the other side for 3 more minutes. Serve warm.

Per Serving: Calories 216 ; Fat 10.4 g; Sodium 311 mg; Carbs 13.5g; Fiber 1g; Sugar 2.36g; Protein 17.99g

Thai Lime Meatballs

Prep time: 5 minutes | Cook time: 15 minutes | Serves: 4

1 lb. ground beef
1 tsp. red Thai curry paste
½ lime, rind and juice

1 tsp. Chinese spice
2 tsp. lemongrass, finely chopped
1 tbsp. sesame oil

1. In a bowl, thoroughly combine all of the ingredients. 2. Make 24 meatballs out of the mixture using equal portions. Place them in the cooking basket of the Air Fryer. 3. Place the AirFryer Basket onto the Baking Pan. AirFry in rack Position 2. 4. Set the Function Dial to AirFry. 5. Set Temperature Dial to 380°F. Then turn the ON/Oven Timer dial to 10 minutes to turn on the oven and begin AirFrying. 6. Before serving with your preferred dipping sauce, flip them and cook for an additional 5 minutes on the other side.

Per Serving: Calories 277 ; Fat 16.0 g; Sodium 70 mg; Carbs 1.03g; Fiber 0.3g; Sugar 0.11g; Protein 30.3g

Herbed Fillet Mignon

Prep time: 5 minutes | Cook time: 13 minutes | Serves: 4

½ lb. filet mignon
Sea salt and ground black pepper, to taste
½ tsp. cayenne pepper
1 tsp. dried basil
1 tsp. dried rosemary

1 tsp. dried thyme
1 tbsp. sesame oil
1 small-sized egg, well-whisked
½ cup friendly breadcrumbs

1. Sprinkle the salt, black pepper, cayenne, basil, rosemary, and thyme over the fillet mignon. Apply a thin layer of sesame oil to the surface. 2. Place the egg on a wide plate. 3. Place the welcoming breadcrumbs on a different platter. 4. Using the egg, coat the fillet mignon. It is rolled in the crumbs. Transfer to the AirFryer Basket. 5. Place the AirFryer Basket onto the Baking Pan. AirFry in rack Position 2. 6.Set the Function Dial to AirFry. 7.Set Temperature Dial to 360°F. Then turn the ON/Oven Timer dial to 10-13 minutes to turn on the oven and begin AirFrying. 8. Offer a salad alongside.

Per Serving: Calories 145 ; Fat 7.2 g; Sodium 65 mg; Carbs 6.7g; Fiber 1.8g; Sugar 1.88g; Protein 14.9g

Spiced Beef Ribs

Prep time: 10 minutes | Cook time: 8 minutes | Serves: 4

1 lb. meaty beef ribs
3 tbsps. apple cider vinegar
1 cup coriander, finely chopped
1 heaped tbsp. fresh basil leaves, chopped
2 garlic cloves, finely chopped

1 chipotle powder
1 tsp. fennel seeds
1 tsp. hot paprika
Kosher salt and black pepper, to taste
½ cup vegetable oil

1. Wash and dry the ribs first. 2. Cover the ribs with the other ingredients and chill for at least three hours. 3. Take the ribs out of the marinade and place them on the AirFryer Basket of an Air Fryer. 4. Place the AirFryer Basket onto the Baking Pan. AirFry in rack Position 2. 5. Set the Function Dial to AirFry. 6. Set Temperature Dial to 360°F. Then turn the ON/Oven Timer dial to the 8 minutes to turn on the oven and begin AirFrying. 7 Before serving the ribs right away, pour the remaining marinade over them.

Per Serving: Calories 629 ; Fat 61.5 g; Sodium 64 mg; Carbs 3.4g; Fiber 0.7g; Sugar 0.73g; Protein 18.4g

London-Style Steak

Prep time: 5 minutes | Cook time: 30 minutes | Serves: 8

2 lb. London broil
3 large garlic cloves, minced
3 tbsp. balsamic vinegar
3 tbsp. whole-grain mustard

2 tbsp. olive oil
Sea salt and ground black pepper, to taste
½ tsp. dried hot red pepper flakes

1. Clean the London broil and dry it. Use a knife to cut slits in its sides. 2. Combine the remaining ingredients. In the broil, rub this mixture in to thoroughly coat it. Permit to marinade for no less than three hours. Transfer to the AirFryer Basket. 3. Place the AirFryer Basket onto the Baking Pan. AirFry in rack Position 2. 4. Set the Function Dial to AirFry. 5. Set Temperature Dial to 400°F. Then turn the ON/Oven Timer dial to the 15 minutes to turn on the oven and begin AirFrying 6. Before serving, flip it over and cook for a further 10 to 12 minutes.

Per Serving: Calories 282; Fat 13g; Sodium 50 mg; Carbs 4.3g; Fiber 0.4g; Sugar 1.3g; Protein 35.2g

Smoked Beef Roast

Prep time: 5 minutes | Cook time: 45 minutes | Serves: 8

2 lb. roast beef, at room temperature
2 tbsps. extra-virgin olive oil
1 tsp. sea salt flakes
1 tsp. black pepper, preferably freshly ground

1 tsp. smoked paprika
Few dashes of liquid smoke
2 jalapeño peppers, thinly sliced

1. Pat the beef dry by using dishtowels. 2. Rub the meat with extra virgin olive oil and spices. 3. Use liquid smoke to cover. Transfer to the AirFryer Basket. 4. Place the AirFryer Basket onto the Baking Pan. AirFry in rack Position 2. 5. Set the Function Dial to AirFry. 6. Set Temperature Dial to 330°F. Then turn the ON/Oven Timer dial to 30 minutes to turn on the oven and begin AirFrying. The roast should cook for an additional 15 minutes after being turned over. 7. When fully cooked, garnish with thinly sliced jalapenos.

Per Serving: Calories 227 ; Fat 11.1 g; Sodium 412 mg; Carbs 1.4g; Fiber 0.4g; Sugar 0.61g; Protein 30.5g

Omelet of Beef and Kale

Prep time: 5 minutes | Cook time: 16 minutes | Serves: 4

Cooking spray
½ lb. leftover beef, coarsely chopped
garlic cloves, pressed
1 cup kale, torn into pieces and wilted
1 tomato, chopped
¼ tsp. sugar

4 eggs, beaten
4 tbsps. heavy cream
½ tsp. turmeric powder
Salt and ground black pepper to taste
⅛ tsp. ground allspice

1. Spray some frying oil onto four ramekins. 2. Evenly distribute the ingredients into each ramekin. 3. Combine thoroughly. Transfer to the AirFryer Basket. 4. Place the AirFryer Basket onto the Baking Pan. AirFry in rack Position 2. 5. Set the Function Dial to AirFry. 6. Set Temperature Dial to 360°F. Then turn the ON/Oven Timer dial to 16 minutes to turn on the oven and begin AirFrying. 7. Serve right away.

Per Serving: Calories 430 ; Fat 29.8 g; Sodium 1292 mg; Carbs 11.2g; Fiber 1.8g; Sugar 7.8g; Protein 28.9g

Beef Cheeseburgers

Prep time: 5 minutes | Cook time:11 minutes | Serves: 4

¾ lb. ground chuck
1 envelope onion soup mix
Kosher salt and freshly ground black pepper, to taste
1 tsp. paprika

slices Monterey-Jack cheese
4 ciabatta rolls
Mustard and pickled salad, to serve

1. Combine the beef chuck, onion soup mix, salt, black pepper, paprika, and other ingredients in a bowl. 2. Divide the ingredients into four equal amounts and shape each one into a patty. Transfer to the AirFryer Basket. 3. Place the AirFryer Basket onto the Baking Pan. AirFry in rack Position 2. 4. Set the Function Dial to AirFry. 5. Set Temperature Dial to 385°F. Then turn the ON/Oven Timer dial to 10 minutes to turn on the oven and begin AirFrying. 6. Place the cheese slices on top of the hamburgers. 7. Cook for a further minute before serving on ciabatta bread with mustard and your preferred pickled salad.

Per Serving: Calories 356 ; Fat 16.6 g; Sodium 627 mg; Carbs 23.1g; Fiber 1.3g; Sugar 2.9g; Protein 27.9g

Crispy Beef

Prep time: 5 minutes | Cook time: 12 minutes | Serves: 1

1 thin beef schnitzel
1 egg, beaten
½ cup friendly bread crumbs

2 tbsps. olive oil
Pepper and salt to taste

1. Combine the bread crumbs, oil, pepper, salt, and other seasonings in a shallow dish. 2. Put the beaten egg in a second shallow dish. 3. Before dredging the schnitzel in the bread crumbs, dip it in the egg. 4. Place the breaded schnitzel in the air fryer basket. Place the AirFryer Basket onto the Baking Pan. AirFry in rack Position 2. 5. Set the Function Dial to AirFry. 6. Set Temperature Dial to 350°F. Then turn the ON/Oven Timer dial to 12 minutes to turn on the oven and begin AirFrying. Serve.

Per Serving: Calories 559; Fat 47.7 g; Sodium 379 mg; Carbs 13.9g; Fiber 1.1g; Sugar 3.9g; Protein 19.7g

Beef Mushrooms Meatloaf

Prep time: 5 minutes | Cook time: 25 minutes | Serves: 4

1 lb. ground beef
1 egg, beaten
1 mushrooms, sliced
1 tbsp. thyme

1 small onion, chopped
3 tbsp. friendly breadcrumbs
Pepper to taste

1. Add each ingredient to a large bowl and thoroughly mix. 2. Place the loaf pan with the meatloaf mixture inside and place the pan in the Air Fryer basket. 3. Place the AirFryer Basket onto the Baking Pan. AirFry in rack Position 2. 4. Set the Function Dial to AirFry. 5. Set Temperature Dial to 400°F. Then turn the ON/Oven Timer dial to 25 minutes to turn on the oven and begin AirFrying. Serve.

Per Serving: Calories 298 ; Fat 15.4 g; Sodium 101 mg; Carbs 5.12g; Fiber 1.1g; Sugar 1.9g; Protein33.1g

Herbed Beef Burgers

Prep time: 5 minutes | Cook time: 25 minutes | Serves: 4

10.5 oz. beef, minced
1 onion, diced
1 tsp. garlic, minced or pureed
1 tsp. tomato, pureed
1 tsp. mustard
1 tsp. basil

1 tsp. mixed herbs
Salt to taste
Pepper to taste
1 oz. cheddar cheese
4 buns
Salad leaves

1. After warming up the Air Fryer, drizzle it with one teaspoon of olive oil. 2. Add the onion dice to the frying and cook until golden brown. 3. Combine all of the ingredients and form into patties and transfer to the AirFryer Basket. Place the AirFryer Basket onto the Baking Pan. AirFry in rack Position 2. 4. Set the Function Dial to AirFry. 5. Set Temperature Dial to 390°F. Then turn the ON/Oven Timer dial to 25 minutes to turn on the oven and begin AirFrying. 6. Place a couple or three onion rings and a tomato puree on two of the buns. The layer of beef should be followed by one slice of cheese. Salad leaves and any additional condiments should be added before securing the sandwich with the remaining buns. 7. Serve with French fries, ketchup, and a cold beverage.

Per Serving: Calories 427 ; Fat 22.6g; Sodium 454 mg; Carbs 36.4g; Fiber 1.5g; Sugar 19g; Protein 19.8g

Tender Beef Chuck with Brussels Sprouts

Prep time: 5 minutes | Cook time: 30 minutes | Serves: 4

1 lb. beef chuck shoulder steak
2 tbsps. vegetable oil
1 tbsp. red wine vinegar
1 tsp. fine sea salt
½ tsp. ground black pepper
1 tsp. smoked paprika

1 tsp. onion powder
½ tsp. garlic powder
½ lb. Brussels sprouts, cleaned and halved
½ tsp. fennel seeds
1 tsp. dried basil
1 tsp. dried sage

1. Coat the meat thoroughly by massaging it with the vegetable oil, wine vinegar, salt, black pepper, paprika, onion powder, and garlic powder. 2. Let the food marinade for at least three hours. Transfer the meat to the AirFryer Basket. 3. Place the AirFryer Basket onto the Baking Pan. AirFry in rack Position 2. 4. Set the Function Dial to AirFry. 5. Set Temperature Dial to 390°F. Then turn the ON/Oven Timer dial to 10 minutes to turn on the oven and begin AirFrying. 6. Add the fennel seeds, basil, and sage to the fryer along with the prepped Brussels sprouts. 7. Reduce the heat to 380°F and simmer the mixture for an additional 5 minutes. 8. Turn off the machine and thoroughly whisk the mixture. Cook for a further ten minutes. 9. Remove the beef, and if necessary or preferred, simmer the vegetables for an additional few minutes. 10. Combine everything and serve it with your preferred sauce.

Per Serving: Calories 253 ; Fat 13.3 g; Sodium 663 mg; Carbs 7.01g; Fiber 2.8g; Sugar 1.9g; Protein 26.3g

Beef Cubes with Roasted Vegetables

Prep time: 5 minutes | Cook time: 18 minutes | Serves: 4

1 lb. top round steak, cut into cubes
2 tbsps. olive oil
1 tbsp. apple cider vinegar
1 tsp. fine sea salt
½ tsp. ground black pepper
1 tsp. shallot powder
¾ tsp. smoked cayenne pepper

½ tsp. garlic powder
¼ tsp. ground cumin
¼ lb. broccoli, cut into florets
¼ lb. mushrooms, sliced
1 tsp. dried basil
1 tsp. celery seeds

1. Evenly cover each piece of the cubed steak with the olive oil, vinegar, salt, black pepper, shallot powder, cayenne pepper, garlic powder, and cumin. 2. Let the food marinade for at least three hours. 3. Place the beef cubes in the Air Fryer cooking basket. 4. Place the AirFryer Basket onto the Baking Pan. AirFry in rack Position 2. 5. Set the Function Dial to AirFry. 6. Set Temperature Dial to 365°F. Then turn the ON/Oven Timer dial to the 12 minutes to turn on the oven and begin AirFrying. 7. After the steak has finished cooking, put it in a bowl. 8. After wiping the frying basket of grease, add the vegetables. They are seasoned with celery and basil seeds. 9. Cook for 5 to 6 minutes at 400°F. Serve the vegetables hot beside the meat.

Per Serving: Calories 342 ; Fat 11.7 g; Sodium 683 mg; Carbs 23.6g; Fiber 4.4g; Sugar 1.12g; Protein 37.8g

Meatballs in Tomato Sauce

Prep time: 5 minutes | Cook time: 12 minutes | Serves: 8

1 lb. ground beef
2 friendly bread slices, crumbled
1 small onion, minced
½ tsp. garlic salt
1 cup tomato sauce

2 cups pasta sauce
1 egg, beaten
2 carrots, shredded
Pepper and salt to taste

1. Mix the ground beef, egg, carrots, bread crumbs, onion, garlic salt, pepper, and salt in a bowl. 2. Equally divide the mixture into portions, then give each portion the shape of a small meatball. Transfer to the AirFryer Basket. 3. Place the AirFryer Basket onto the Baking Pan. AirFry in rack Position 2. 4. Set the Function Dial to AirFry. 5. Set Temperature Dial to 400°F. Then turn the ON/Oven Timer dial to 7 minutes to turn on the oven and begin AirFrying. 6. Place the meatballs in a dish that can be baked and cover with tomato sauce. 7. Place the dish in the Air Fryer basket and cook at 320°F for an additional five minutes. Serve warm.

Per Serving: Calories 217 ; Fat 7.9 g; Sodium 998 mg; Carbs 16.5g; Fiber 4 g; Sugar 7.91g; Protein 18.8g

Ham and Mushroom Omelette

Prep time: 5 minutes | Cook time: 10 minutes | Serves: 9

1 tablespoon flax seeds
¼ teaspoon sea salt
½ teaspoon paprika
1 teaspoon ground black pepper
1 teaspoon olive oil

4-ounces white mushrooms, sliced
½ cup cream cheese
7 eggs
½ cup diced cooked ham

1. Toss the sliced mushrooms with paprika, sea salt, and freshly ground black pepper. 2. Place the cut mushrooms within the olive oil-sprayed air fryer basket tray. 3. Place the AirFryer Basket onto the Baking Pan. AirFry in rack Position 2. 4. Set the Function Dial to AirFry. 5. Set Temperature Dial to 400°F. Then turn the ON/Oven Timer dial to the 3 minutes to turn on the oven and begin AirFrying. 6. Whip the eggs and ham in a small bowl while you wait. 7. Mix the egg mixture well before adding the cream cheese and flax seeds. 8. Over the mushrooms on the air fryer basket tray, pour the omelette. 9. Omelet is gently stirred and cooked for 7 minutes. 10. Using a wooden spatula, remove the cooked omelette from the air fryer basket tray. 11. Serve it warm after slicing it into portions.

Per Serving: Calories 157 ; Fat 12.4 g; Sodium 217 mg; Carbs 2.5g; Fiber 0.5g; Sugar 1.3g; Protein 8.7g

Cream Scrambled Eggs with Bacon

Prep time: 5 minutes | Cook time: 10 minutes | Serves: 4

6-ounces bacon, chopped into small pieces
4 eggs
5 tablespoons heavy cream
1 teaspoon ground black pepper

1 teaspoon salt
½ teaspoon nutmeg
1 teaspoon paprika
1 tablespoon butter

1. Salt the bacon once it has been diced into small bits. Put the bacon in the air fryer basket. 2.Place the AirFryer Basket onto the Baking Pan. AirFry in rack Position 2. 3. Set the Function Dial to AirFry. 4. Set Temperature Dial to 360°F. Then turn the ON/Oven Timer dial to 5 minutes to turn on the oven and begin AirFrying ,cook the chopped bacon in an air fryer that has been heated to 360°F. 5. In the meantime, whisk the eggs by hand and beating them in a bowl. 6. Add ground black pepper, nutmeg, and paprika to the egg mixture while whisking. 7. Place the diced bacon and butter in a bowl and then top with the egg mixture. 8. Cook for two minutes after adding the heavy cream. 9. After that, simmer the dish for an additional three minutes while continuing to stir the mixture with a spatula until scrambled eggs form. 10. Serve the dish warm after transferring it to serving plates.

Per Serving: Calories 356 ; Fat 32.2 g; Sodium 1337 mg; Carbs 5.14g; Fiber 1.5g; Sugar 1.2g; Protein 14.1g

Breakfast Pork Sticks with Cheese

Prep time: 5 minutes | Cook time:10 minutes | Serves: 4

10-ounce pork fillet
1 tablespoon olive oil
½ teaspoon salt
1 teaspoon paprika
1 teaspoon apple cider vinegar

1 teaspoon oregano
1 teaspoon nutmeg
¼ teaspoon ground ginger
1 teaspoon basil, dried
5-ounces Parmesan cheese, shredded

1. Thick slices of pork fillet should be cut. In a small bowl, whisk together the salt, paprika, oregano, nutmeg, and ginger. 2. The spice combination should be sprinkled over the pork strips. 3. Sprinkle apple cider vinegar over the pork strips. Transfer to the AirFryer Basket. 4. Place the AirFryer Basket onto the Baking Pan. AirFry in rack Position 2. 5. Set the Function Dial to AirFry. 6. Set Temperature Dial to 380°F. Then turn the ON/Oven Timer dial to 5 minutes to turn on the oven and begin AirFrying , then flip them over and cook for an additional four minutes. 7. Add the parmesan cheese and fry the pork strips for an additional minute. Serve the pork strips right away after removing them from the air fryer.

Per Serving: Calories 329 ; Fat 20.9 g; Sodium 973 mg; Carbs 5.8g; Fiber 0.4g; Sugar 0.12g; Protein 29.9g

Minty Lamb Racks

Prep time: 5 minutes | Cook time: 15 minutes | Serves: 2

2 racks of lamb
1 bunch of fresh mint
Salt and pepper to taste

⅓ cup extra-virgin olive oil
1 tablespoon honey
2 garlic cloves

1. Blend all the ingredients with the exception of the lamb, puree into sauce. 2. Lamb racks should be chopped into small pieces from top to bottom, between the bones, and then tied into a crown shape with kitchen twine. Spread sauce liberally on the rack. Transfer to the AirFryer Basket. 3. Place the AirFryer Basket onto the Baking Pan. AirFry in rack Position 2. 4. Set the Function Dial to AirFry. Set Temperature Dial to 390°F. Then turn the ON/Oven Timer dial to 15 minutes to turn on the oven and begin AirFrying ,remove the air fryer lid and add extra sauce to the rack. 5. Serve with freshly chopped vegetables and mashed potatoes.

Per Serving: Calories 298 ; Fat 15.4 g; Sodium 101 mg; Carbs 5.12g; Fiber 1.1g; Sugar 1.9g; Protein33.1g

Garlicky Lamb Chops

Prep time: 10 minutes | Cook time: 22 minutes | Serves: 4

1 tablespoon + 2 tablespoons olive oil, divided
4 lamb chops
Pinch of black pepper

1 tablespoon dried thyme
1 garlic clove

1. Cook the garlic with 1 tablespoon of olive oil at 390°F for 10 minutes in your air fryer. Combine remaining olive oil with the thyme and pepper. 2. Add the squeezed roasted garlic to the thyme and oil combination. Over the lamb chops, brush the mixture. 3. Transfer the lamb chops to the AirFryer Basket. Place the AirFryer Basket onto the Baking Pan. AirFry in rack Position 2. 4. Set the Function Dial to AirFry. Set Temperature Dial to 390°F. Then turn the ON/Oven Timer dial to 12 minutes to turn on the oven and begin AirFrying. Serve.

Per Serving: Calories 151 ; Fat 13 g; Sodium 33 mg; Carbs 0.55g; Fiber 0.2g; Sugar 0.01g; Protein 8.5g

Nut-Crusted Rack of Lamb

Prep time: 15 minutes | Cook time: 35 minutes | Serves: 4

1 garlic clove, minced
1⅓ lbs. rack of lamb
1 tablespoon olive oil
Salt and pepper to taste
1 tablespoon breadcrumbs

Macadamia Crust:
3-ounces macadamia nuts, raw and unsalted
1 egg, beaten
1 tablespoon fresh rosemary, chopped

1. Garlic and olive oil should be combined in a small bowl. 2. Salt and pepper should be brushed on the lamb all over. 3. Macadamia nuts should be chopped in a food processor and combined with breadcrumbs and rosemary. Make sure the nuts don't become a paste. 4. Add egg and mix. 5. Apply nut mixture to lamb. Transfer the lamb to the AirFryer Basket. 6. Place the AirFryer Basket onto the Baking Pan. AirFry in rack Position 2. 7. Set the Function Dial to AirFry. 8. Set Temperature Dial to 220°F. Then turn the ON/Oven Timer dial to 30 minutes to turn on the oven and begin AirFrying. 9. Increase the heat to 390°F and cook the food for an additional five minutes. 10. Remove the meat and loosely cover it with foil for 10 minutes. Serve hot.

Per Serving: Calories 469 ; Fat 35 g; Sodium 141 mg; Carbs 5.82g; Fiber 2.2g; Sugar 1.82g; Protein 35.5g

Pork and Pumpkin Empanadas

Prep time: 5 minutes | Cook time: 30 minutes | Serves: 4

2 tablespoons olive oil
1 package of 10 empanada discs
Black pepper to taste
1 teaspoon salt
½ teaspoon dried thyme
½ teaspoon cinnamon

1 red chile pepper, minced
3 tablespoons water
1½ cups pumpkin puree
1 lb. ground pork
½ onion, diced

1. Warm up some olive oil in a pan. 2. Cook the pork and onions for about five minutes. Then, add the pumpkin, chile pepper, cinnamon, water, thyme, salt, and pepper after removing the fat. 3. Good stirring. To enable the flavours to meld, cook for 10 minutes. 4. Set apart for cooling. 5. Spread the empanada discs from the packet out on your tabletop after opening them. 6. Add a few teaspoons of filling to each before folding the sides toward the centre to create a Cornish pasty shape. 7. Apply olive oil, then repeat with the remaining items. On your air fryer basket, put the empanadas, Place the AirFryer Basket onto the Baking Pan. AirFry in rack Position 2. 8. Set the Function Dial to AirFry. 9. Set Temperature Dial to 370°F. Then turn the ON/Oven Timer dial to 15 minutes to turn on the oven and begin AirFrying. Once done, serve.

Per Serving: Calories 826 ; Fat 58.5g; Sodium 1003 mg; Carbs 33.3g; Fiber 4.8g; Sugar 7.18g; Protein 45.4g

Spicy Pork with Peanut Sauce

Prep time: 5 minutes | Cook time: 12 minutes | Serves: 4

1 teaspoon ground ginger
2 teaspoons hot pepper sauce
2 cloves garlic, crushed
3 tablespoons sweet soy sauce
3½ ounces unsalted peanuts, ground

¾ cup coconut milk
1 teaspoon ground coriander
2 tablespoons vegetable oil
14-ounces lean pork chops, in cubes of 1-inch

1. Combine spicy sauce, ginger, half a garlic clove, oil, and soy sauce in a sizable mixing bowl. 2. Put the meat in the mixture and let it marinate for 15 minutes. 3. Put the meat in the air fryer's basket. 4. Place the AirFryer Basket onto the Baking Pan. AirFry in rack Position 2. 5. Set the Function Dial to AirFry. 6. Set Temperature Dial to 390°F. Then turn the ON/Oven Timer dial to 12 minutes to turn on the oven and begin AirFrying. 7. Halfway through the cooking period, flip. 8. Heat up the oil in a skillet to make the peanut sauce. 9. Cook for 5 minutes, stirring frequently, after adding the garlic and coriander. Bring to a boil the coconut milk, peanuts, spicy sauce, and soy sauce in the pan. often stir. 10. Take the pork out of the air fryer, cover it with sauce, and serve it warm.

Per Serving: Calories 564 ; Fat 43 g; Sodium 245 mg; Carbs 13.6g; Fiber 3.8g; Sugar 6.2g; Protein33.9g

Crumbed Pork with Tomato Pesto

Prep time: 5 minutes | Cook time: 20 minutes | Serves: 2

½ cup milk
1 egg
1 cup breadcrumbs
1 tablespoon parmesan cheese, grated
¼ bunch of thyme, chopped
1 teaspoon pine nuts
¼ cup semi-dried tomatoes

½ cup almond flour
2 pork cutlets
1 lemon, zested
Sea salt and black pepper to taste
Basil leaves
1 tablespoon olive oil

1. In a bowl, whisk together the milk and egg. 2. Set bowl aside. Breadcrumbs, parmesan, thyme, lemon zest, salt, and pepper should all be combined in another bowl. 3. In another bowl, add the flour. 4. Pork cutlets are dipped in flour, egg and milk mixture, and then breadcrumb mixture. Transfer the pork to the AirFryer Basket. 5. Place the AirFryer Basket onto the Baking Pan. AirFry in rack Position 2. 6. Set the Function Dial to AirFry. 7. Set Temperature Dial to 360°F. Then turn the ON/Oven Timer dial to 20 minutes to turn on the oven and begin AirFrying. 8. Cook the pork in the basket until it is golden and crisp. To make the pesto, put the basil leaves, tomatoes, pine nuts, and olive oil in a food processor. 9. For 20 seconds, blend. When the pork is done, serve it with pesto and your preferred salad.

Per Serving: Calories 595 ; Fat 33.7 g; Sodium 314 mg; Carbs 21.4g; Fiber 2.5g; Sugar 8.7g; Protein 50.9g

Spicy Pork Loin with Potatoes

Prep time: 5 minutes | Cook time: 25 minutes | Serves: 2

2 lbs. pork loin
½ teaspoon garlic powder
½ teaspoon red pepper flakes

½ teaspoon black pepper
2 large potatoes, chunked

1. Garlic powder, red pepper flakes, salt, and pepper should all be added to the pork loin. 2. Put the potatoes and pork loin in the air fryer basket 3. Place the AirFryer Basket onto the Baking Pan. AirFry in rack Position 2. 4. Set the Function Dial to AirFry. 5. Set Temperature Dial to 370°F. Then turn the ON/Oven Timer dial to 25 minutes to turn on the oven and begin AirFrying, cook. 6. Take the potatoes and pork loin out of the air fryer. Slice the pork loin after it has cooled, then indulge.

Per Serving: Calories 1241 ; Fat 50.5 g; Sodium 273 mg; Carbs 66.5g; Fiber 8.5g; Sugar 3.4g; Protein 124g

Herbed Pork Ribs

Prep time: 5 minutes | Cook time: 12 minutes | Serves: 4

4 country-style pork ribs, trimmed of excess fat
Salt and black pepper to taste
1 teaspoon dried marjoram
1 teaspoon garlic powder

1 teaspoon thyme
2 teaspoons dry mustard
3 tablespoons coconut oil
3 tablespoons cornstarch

1. Combine everything in a bowl, excluding the pork ribs. 2. Rub the mixture into the ribs after soaking them. 3. Transfer to the AirFryer Basket. Place the AirFryer Basket onto the Baking Pan. AirFry in rack Position 2. 4. Set the Function Dial to AirFry. Set Temperature Dial to 400°F. Then turn the ON/Oven Timer dial to 12 minutes to turn on the oven and begin AirFrying. 5. Cook. Dispense and savour!

Per Serving: Calories 396 ; Fat 21.4 g; Sodium 162 mg; Carbs 7.3g; Fiber 0.5g; Sugar 0.6g; Protein 41.3g

Chapter 5 Fish and Seafood

Swordfish Steaks with Mint and Lemon

Prep time: 5 minutes | Cook time: 10 minutes | Serves: 4

1-pound swordfish steaks
2 tablespoons olive oil
2 tablespoons fresh mint leaves, chopped
3 tablespoons fresh lemon juice

1 teaspoon garlic powder
½ teaspoon shallot powder
Sea salt and freshly ground black pepper, to taste

1. Swordfish steaks should be mixed with the remaining ingredients and put in a cooking basket for an Air Fryer that has been lightly oiled. 2. Place the AirFryer Basket onto the Baking Pan. AirFry in rack Position 2. 2. Set the Function Dial to AirFry. 3. Set Temperature Dial to 400°F. Then turn the ON/Oven Timer dial to 10 minutes to turn on the oven and begin AirFrying, turning them over halfway through.

Per Serving: Calories 229 ; Fat 14.3 g; Sodium 93 mg; Carbs 1.4g; Fiber 0.2g; Sugar 0.35g; Protein 22.4g

Mackerel Patties with English Muffins

Prep time: 5 minutes | Cook time: 15 minutes | Serves: 4

1-pound mackerel fillet, boneless and chopped
1 tablespoon olive oil
½ onion, chopped
2 garlic cloves, crushed
1 teaspoon hot paprika

1 tablespoon fresh cilantro, chopped
2 tablespoons fresh parsley, chopped
Sea salt and ground black pepper, to taste
4 English muffins, toasted

1. In a bowl, combine all the ingredients minus the English muffins. Four patties made from the mixture should be placed in a frying basket for an Air Fryer that has been lightly greased. 2. Place the AirFryer Basket onto the Baking Pan. AirFry in rack Position 2. 3. Set the Function Dial to AirFry. 4. Set Temperature Dial to 400°F. Then turn the ON/Oven Timer dial to 14 minutes to turn on the oven and begin AirFrying, flipping them halfway through. 5. Enjoy your serving on English muffins!

Per Serving: Calories 291 ; Fat 6.9 g; Sodium 384 mg; Carbs 28.8g; Fiber 3.3g; Sugar 2.14g; Protein 28.7g

Herbed Calamari Rings

Prep time: 5 minutes | Cook time: 5 minutes | Serves: 4

1 pound calamari, sliced into rings
2 garlic cloves, minced
1 teaspoon red pepper flakes
2 tablespoons dry white wine
2 tablespoons olive oil

2 tablespoons fresh lemon juice
1 teaspoon basil, chopped
1 teaspoon dill, chopped
1 teaspoon parsley, chopped
Coarse sea salt and freshly cracked black pepper, to taste

1. Toss all ingredients in an Air Fryer cooking basket that has been lightly oiled. 2. Place Calamari into the AirFryer Basket onto the Baking Pan. AirFry in rack Position 2. 3. Set the Function Dial to AirFry. 4. Set Temperature Dial to 400°F. Then turn the ON/Oven Timer dial to 5 minutes to turn on the oven and begin AirFrying. Once done, serve.

Per Serving: Calories 441 ; Fat 37.4 g; Sodium 79 mg; Carbs 6.8g; Fiber 0.4g; Sugar 0.8g; Protein 19.5g

Smoked Paprika Pollock Hamburgers

Prep time: 5 minutes | Cook time: 15 minutes | Serves: 4

1 pound pollock, chopped
1 teaspoon chili sauce
Sea salt and ground black pepper, to taste
4 tablespoons all-purpose flour

1 teaspoon smoked paprika
2 tablespoons olive oil
4 ciabatta buns

1. In a bowl, combine all the ingredients minus the ciabatta rolls. Four patties made from the mixture should be placed in a frying basket for an Air Fryer that has been lightly greased. 2. Place the AirFryer Basket onto the Baking Pan. AirFry in rack Position 2. 3. Set the Function Dial to AirFry. Set Temperature Dial to 400°F. Then turn the ON/Oven Timer dial to 14 minutes to turn on the oven and begin AirFrying, flipping them halfway through. 4. Enjoy your meal on hamburger buns!

Per Serving: Calories 476 ; Fat 29.1 g; Sodium 598 mg; Carbs 34.7g; Fiber 2g; Sugar 17.9g; Protein 19.4g

Spicy Herbed Squid with Cheese

Prep time: 5 minutes | Cook time: 5 minutes | Serves: 4

1½ pounds small squid tubes
2 tablespoons butter, melted
1 chili pepper, chopped
2 garlic cloves, minced
1 teaspoon red pepper flakes

Sea salt and ground black pepper, to taste
¼ cup dry white wine
2 tablespoons fresh lemon juice
1 teaspoon Mediterranean herb mix
2 tablespoons Parmigiano-Reggiano cheese, grated

1. All ingredients should be combined in a lightly greased Air Fryer cooking basket, with the exception of the Parmigiano-Reggiano cheese. 2. Place AirFryer Basket onto the Baking Pan. AirFry in rack Position 2. 3. Set the Function Dial to AirFry. 4. Set Temperature Dial to 400°F. Then turn the ON/Oven Timer dial to 5 minutes to turn on the oven and begin AirFrying. Tossing the basket halfway through. 5. Place the cheese on top of the warm squid.

Per Serving: Calories 251 ; Fat 10.3 g; Sodium 279 mg; Carbs 9.01g; Fiber 0.4g; Sugar 1.45g; Protein 29.3g

Delicious Fried Shrimp

Prep time: 5 minutes | Cook time: 10 minutes | Serves: 4

1½ pounds shrimp, cleaned and deveined
½ cup all-purpose flour
½ teaspoon shallot powder
½ teaspoon garlic powder
1 teaspoon red pepper flakes, crushed

Sea salt and ground black pepper, to taste
2 large eggs
1 cup crackers, crushed
½ cup Parmesan cheese, grated

1. Combine the spices and flour in a small bowl. In the second bowl, whisk the eggs, and in the third, combine the cheese and crackers. 2. The shrimp are coated thoroughly on all sides after being dipped in the flour mixture, whisked eggs, and finally the cracker/cheese mixture. 3. Put the shrimp in an Air Fryer cooking basket that has been generously oiled. 4. Place the AirFryer Basket onto the Baking Pan. AirFry in rack Position 2. 5. Set the Function Dial to AirFry. 6. Set Temperature Dial to 400°F. Then turn the ON/Oven Timer dial to 10 minutes to turn on the oven and begin AirFrying. Tossing the basket halfway through.

Per Serving: Calories 317 ; Fat 37.4 g; Sodium 79 mg; Carbs 6.8g; Fiber 0.4g; Sugar 0.8g; Protein 19.5g

Air Fried Sea Bass

Prep time: 5 minutes | Cook time: 10 minutes | Serves: 3

2 tablespoons butter, room temperature
1 pound sea bass
¼ cup dry white wine
¼ cup all-purpose flour

Sea salt and ground black pepper, to taste
1 teaspoon mustard seeds
1 teaspoon fennel seeds
2 cloves garlic, minced

1. Place the fish and the additional ingredients in a cooking basket for an Air Fryer that has been lightly greased. 2. Place the AirFryer Basket onto the Baking Pan. AirFry in rack Position 2. 3. Set the Function Dial to AirFry. 4. Set Temperature Dial to 400°F. Then turn the ON/Oven Timer dial to 10 minutes to turn on the oven and begin AirFrying, flipping them halfway through.

Per Serving: Calories 294 ; Fat 13.1 g; Sodium 312 mg; Carbs 10.7g; Fiber 0.9g; Sugar 0.9g; Protein 31.7g

Lemony Salmon Fillets with Herbs

Prep time: 5 minutes | Cook time: 12 minutes | Serves: 4

1½ pounds salmon fillets
2 sprigs fresh rosemary
1 tablespoon fresh basil
1 tablespoon fresh thyme
1 tablespoon fresh dill

1 small lemon, juiced
2 tablespoons olive oil
Sea salt and ground black pepper, to taste
1 teaspoon stone-ground mustard
2 cloves garlic, chopped

1. Place the salmon in a cooking basket for an Air Fryer after tossing it with the additional ingredients. 2. Place the AirFryer Basket onto the Baking Pan. AirFry in rack Position 2. 3. Set the Function Dial to AirFry. 4. Set Temperature Dial to 380°F. Then turn the ON/Oven Timer dial to 12 minutes to turn on the oven and begin AirFrying, flipping them over halfway through. 5. Serve right away and delight in!

Per Serving: Calories 339 ; Fat 19.4 g; Sodium 739 mg; Carbs 3.7g; Fiber 0.9g; Sugar 0.93g; Protein 35.9g

Spicy Calamari

½ cup milk
1 cup all-purpose flour
2 tablespoons olive oil
1 teaspoon turmeric powder

Sea salt flakes and ground black, to taste
1 teaspoon paprika
1 red chili, minced
1 pound calamari, cut into rings

1. Mix the milk, flour, olive oil, salt, black pepper, paprika, turmeric powder, and red chili well in a mixing bowl. 2. Now, coat your calamari by dipping it into the flour mixture. 3. Place Calamari into the AirFryer Basket onto the Baking Pan. AirFry in rack Position 2. 4. Set the Function Dial to AirFry. 5. Set Temperature Dial to 380°F. Then turn the ON/Oven Timer dial to 5 minutes to turn on the oven and begin AirFrying, flipping them halfway through.

.Per Serving: Calories 400 ; Fat 20.6 g; Sodium 120 mg; Carbs 27.2 g; Fiber 1.4g; Sugar 1.76g; Protein 26.2g

Shrimp and Veggie Rolls

1-pound shrimp, peeled and chilled
1 teaspoon olive oil
1 stalks celery, sliced
1 English cucumber, sliced
1 shallot, sliced
1 tablespoon fresh dill, roughly chopped
Coarse sea salt and lemon pepper, to taste
4 hoagie rolls

1 tablespoon fresh parsley, roughly chopped
1 tablespoon fresh lime juice
1 tablespoon apple cider vinegar
½ cup mayonnaise
1 teaspoon Creole seasoning mix
1½ teaspoons Dijon mustard

1. Put the shrimp and oil in the frying basket of the Air Fryer. 2. Place AirFryer Basket onto the Baking Pan. AirFry in rack Position 2. 3. Set the Function Dial to AirFry. 4. Set Temperature Dial to 400°F. Then turn the ON/Oven Timer dial to 6 minutes to turn on the oven and begin AirFrying, tossing the basket halfway through. 5. Mix the other ingredients in a bowl with the shrimp; spoon the mixture onto the prepared hoagie rolls.

Per Serving: Calories 333 ; Fat 13.4 g; Sodium 655 mg; Carbs 24.4g; Fiber 1.9g; Sugar 3.39g; Protein 29.2g

Sea Bass in Italian Fashion

1-pound sea bass
2 garlic cloves, minced
2 tablespoons olive oil

1 tablespoon Italian seasoning mix
Sea salt and ground black pepper, to taste
¼ cup dry white wine

1. Place the fish and the additional ingredients in a cooking basket for an Air Fryer that has been lightly greased. 2. Place AirFryer Basket onto the Baking Pan. AirFry in rack Position 2. 3. Set the Function Dial to AirFry. 4. Set Temperature Dial to 400°F. Then turn the ON/Oven Timer dial to 10 minutes to turn on the oven and begin AirFrying, tossing the basket halfway through.

Per Serving: Calories 248 ; Fat 13.9 g; Sodium 366 mg; Carbs 2.9g; Fiber 0.5g; Sugar 0.86g; Protein 27.8g

Fried Calamari with Mustard

Prep time: 5 minutes | Cook time: 5 minutes | Serves: 4

2 cups flour
Sea salt and ground black pepper, to taste
1 teaspoon garlic, minced

1 tablespoon mustard
2 tablespoons olive oil
1 pound calamari, sliced into rings

1. Combine the flour, salt, black pepper, garlic, mustard, and olive oil in a mixing bowl until well-combined. 2. Now, coat your calamari by dipping it into the flour mixture. 3. Place AirFryer Basket onto the Baking Pan. AirFry in rack Position 2. 4. Set the Function Dial to AirFry. 5. Set Temperature Dial to 400°F. Then turn the ON/Oven Timer dial to 5 minutes to turn on the oven and begin AirFrying, tossing the basket halfway through.

Per Serving: Calories 645 ; Fat 38.1 g; Sodium 122 mg; Carbs 49.22g; Fiber 2g; Sugar 0.7g; Protein 25.5g

Crispy Fish fingers

Prep time: 5 minutes | Cook time: 10 minutes | Serves: 4

½ cup all-purpose flour
Sea salt and ground black pepper
1 teaspoon cayenne pepper
½ teaspoon onion powder
1 tablespoon Italian parsley, chopped

1 teaspoon garlic powder
1 egg, whisked
½ cup Pecorino Romano cheese, grated
1-pound monkfish, sliced into strips

1. Combine the cheese, egg, flour, and spices in a small bowl. Fish strips should be well covered on all sides after being dipped in the batter. 2. Place the fish strips in the frying basket of the Air Fryer. 3. Place AirFryer Basket onto the Baking Pan. AirFry in rack Position 2. 4. Set the Function Dial to AirFry. 5. Set Temperature Dial to 400°F. Then turn the ON/Oven Timer dial to 10 minutes to turn on the oven and begin AirFrying, tossing the basket halfway through.

Per Serving: Calories 238 ; Fat 7.8 g; Sodium 274 mg; Carbs 16.1g; Fiber 0.9g; Sugar 0.88g; Protein 24.3g

Catfish Croquettes

Prep time: 5 minutes | Cook time: 15 minutes | Serves: 4

1-pound catfish, skinless, boneless and chopped
2 tablespoons olive oil
2 cloves garlic, minced
1 small onion, minced

¼ cup all-purpose flour
Sea salt and ground black pepper, to taste
½ cup breadcrumbs

1. In a bowl, combine each item. Create bite-sized balls out of the mixture and put them in the frying basket of an Air Fryer that has been lightly greased. 2. Place AirFryer Basket onto the Baking Pan. AirFry in rack Position 2. 3. Set the Function Dial to AirFry. 4. Set Temperature Dial to 400°F. Then turn the ON/Oven Timer dial to 14 minutes to turn on the oven and begin AirFrying, tossing the basket halfway through.

.**Per Serving:** Calories 221 ; Fat 10.2 g; Sodium 72 mg; Carbs 11.3g; Fiber 0.8g; Sugar 1.6g; Protein 20.2g

Fried Breaded Shrimps

1 cup all-purpose flour
1 teaspoon Old Bay seasoning
Sea salt and lemon pepper, to taste

½ cup buttermilk
1 cup seasoned breadcrumbs
1½ pounds shrimp, peeled and deveined

1. Combine the flour, spices, and buttermilk in a small basin. The second bowl should contain the seasoned breadcrumbs. 2. The shrimp should be thoroughly coated on all sides after being dipped in the flour mixture and breadcrumbs. Transfer the shrimp to the AirFryer Basket. 3. Place AirFryer Basket onto the Baking Pan. AirFry in rack Position 2. 4. Set the Function Dial to AirFry. 5. Set Temperature Dial to 400°F. Then turn the ON/Oven Timer dial to 10 minutes to turn on the oven and begin AirFrying, tossing the basket halfway through.

Per Serving: Calories 407 ; Fat 2.9 g; Sodium 4002 mg; Carbs 44.2g; Fiber 5.4g; Sugar 5.2g; Protein 40.5g

Mediterranean Mackerel Fish Pita Wraps.

1-pound mackerel fish fillets
2 tablespoons olive oil
1 tablespoon Mediterranean seasoning mix
½ teaspoon chili powder

Sea salt and freshly ground black pepper, to taste
2 ounces Feta cheese, crumbled
4 (6-½ inch) tortillas

1. Place the fish fillets in a frying basket for an Air Fryer that has been lightly oiled. 2. Place AirFryer Basket onto the Baking Pan. AirFry in rack Position 2. 3. Set the Function Dial to AirFry. 4. Set Temperature Dial to 400°F. Then turn the ON/Oven Timer dial to 14 minutes to turn on the oven and begin AirFrying, tossing the basket halfway through. 5. Pitas should be warm when assembled with the chopped fish and other toppings.

Per Serving: Calories 362 ; Fat 14.8 g; Sodium 807 mg; Carbs 26.06g; Fiber 1.6g; Sugar 2.4g; Protein 28.8g

Butter Shrimp with Cilantro

1-pound jumbo shrimp
2 tablespoons butter, at room temperature
Coarse sea salt and lemon pepper, to taste

2 tablespoons fresh cilantro, chopped
2 tablespoons fresh chives, chopped
2 garlic cloves, crushed

1. Toss all ingredients in an Air Fryer cooking basket that has been lightly oiled. 2. Place the AirFryer Basket onto the Baking Pan. AirFry in rack Position 2. Set the Function Dial to AirFry. 3. Set Temperature Dial to 400°F. Then turn the ON/Oven Timer dial to 8 minutes to turn on the oven and begin AirFrying, tossing the basket halfway through.

Per Serving: Calories 167 ; Fat 7.3 g; Sodium 1033 mg; Carbs 0.5g; Fiber 0.1g; Sugar 0.05g; Protein 23.3g

Sea Scallops with Rosemary

Prep time: 5 minutes | Cook time: 7 minutes | Serves: 4

1½ pounds sea scallops
4 tablespoons butter, melted
1 tablespoon garlic, minced

Sea salt and ground black pepper, to season
2 rosemary sprigs, leaves picked and chopped
4 tablespoons dry white wine

1. Toss all ingredients in an Air Fryer cooking basket that has been lightly oiled. 2. Place the AirFryer Basket onto the Baking Pan. AirFry in rack Position 2. Set the Function Dial to AirFry. 3. Set Temperature Dial to 400°F. Then turn the ON/Oven Timer dial to 7 minutes to turn on the oven and begin AirFrying, tossing the basket halfway through.

Per Serving: Calories 343 ; Fat 13.1 g; Sodium 1227 mg; Carbs 20.5g; Fiber 0.5g; Sugar 0.6g; Protein 36.3g

Squid Stuffed with Sausage

Prep time: 5 minutes | Cook time: 5 minutes | Serves: 4

2 tablespoons olive oil, divided, or as needed
1 small onion, chopped
2 cloves garlic, minced
1 tablespoon fresh parsley, chopped

1 small Italian pepper, chopped
Sea salt and ground black pepper, to taste
4 ounces beef sausage, crumbled
1-pound squid tubes, cleaned

1. Combine the sausage, olive oil, onion, garlic, parsley, Italian pepper, salt, and black pepper in a mixing bowl. 2. Put the sausage filling inside the squid tubes, and then fasten them with toothpicks. 3. Put them in an Air Fryer cooking basket that has been lightly greased. 4. Place the AirFryer Basket onto the Baking Pan. AirFry in rack Position 2. Set the Function Dial to AirFry. 5. Set Temperature Dial to 400°F. Then turn the ON/Oven Timer dial to 5 minutes to turn on the oven and begin AirFrying, tossing the basket halfway through.

Per Serving: Calories 255 ; Fat 13.8 g; Sodium 305 mg; Carbs 10.6g; Fiber 1.5g; Sugar 1.9g; Protein 23.6g

Haddock Cheeseburgers

Prep time: 5 minutes | Cook time: 15 minutes | Serves: 4

1-pound haddock, boneless and
¼ cup all-purpose flour
2 eggs

½ cup parmesan cheese, grated
½ cup breadcrumbs
4 brioche buns

1. In a bowl, combine all the ingredients minus the brioche buns. Four patties made from the mixture should be placed in a frying basket for an Air Fryer that has been lightly greased. 2. Place the AirFryer Basket onto the Baking Pan. AirFry in rack Position 2. Set the Function Dial to AirFry. 3. Set Temperature Dial to 400°F. Then turn the ON/Oven Timer dial to 14 minutes to turn on the oven and begin AirFrying, tossing the basket halfway through. 4. Enjoy your meal on hamburger buns!

Per Serving: Calories 535 ; Fat 26.3 g; Sodium 738 mg; Carbs 41.9g; Fiber 1.1g; Sugar 17.3g; Protein 30.6g

Shrimp and Herbed Celery Salad

Prep time: 5 minutes | Cook time: 6 minutes | Serves: 4

1½ pounds shrimp, peeled and deveined
1 tablespoon olive oil
Sea salt and freshly ground black pepper, to taste
1 teaspoon fresh dill, chopped
1 teaspoon fresh basil, chopped
1 tablespoon fresh parsley, chopped

2 tablespoons chives, chopped
1 bell pepper, seeded and chopped
1 celery stalk, trimmed and chopped
½ cup mayonnaise
1 teaspoon stone-ground mustard
1 tablespoon fresh lime juice

1. Put the shrimp and oil in the frying basket of the Air Fryer. 2. Place the AirFryer Basket onto the Baking Pan. AirFry in rack Position 2. Set the Function Dial to AirFry. 3. Set Temperature Dial to 400°F. Then turn the ON/Oven Timer dial to 6 minutes to turn on the oven and begin AirFrying, tossing the basket halfway through. 4. In a salad dish, add the shrimp and the remaining ingredients. Gently mix to blend. Serve thoroughly cold.

Per Serving: Calories 308 ; Fat 15.5 g; Sodium 1717 mg; Carbs 3.07g; Fiber 0.9 g; Sugar 1.02g; Protein 37.1g

Lemony Spiced Calamari

Prep time: 5 minutes | Cook time: 5 minutes | Serves: 4

1 pound calamari, sliced into rings
Sea salt and ground black pepper, to taste
1 teaspoon cayenne pepper

1 teaspoon garlic powder
2 tablespoons lemon juice
2 tablespoons olive oil

1. Toss all ingredients in an Air Fryer cooking basket that has been lightly oiled. 2. Place the AirFryer Basket onto the Baking Pan. AirFry in rack Position 2. Set the Function Dial to AirFry. 3. Set Temperature Dial to 400°F. Then turn the ON/Oven Timer dial to 5 minutes to turn on the oven and begin AirFrying, tossing the basket halfway through.

Per Serving: Calories 420 ; Fat 37.4 g; Sodium 79 mg; Carbs 2.4g; Fiber 0.4g; Sugar 0.83g; Protein 19.1g

Sea Scallops and Vegetable Salad

Prep time: 5 minutes | Cook time: 7 minutes | Serves: 4

1½ pounds sea scallops
Sea salt and ground black pepper, to taste
2 tablespoons olive oil
1 tablespoon balsamic vinegar
2 garlic cloves, minced

2 teaspoons fresh tarragon, minced
1 teaspoon Dijon mustard
1 cup mixed baby greens
1 small tomato, diced

1. Cooking basket for an Air Fryer should be lightly greased before adding the scallops, salt, and black pepper. 2. Place the AirFryer Basket onto the Baking Pan. AirFry in rack Position 2. Set the Function Dial to AirFry. 3. Set Temperature Dial to 400°F. Then turn the ON/Oven Timer dial to 7 minutes to turn on the oven and begin AirFrying, tossing the basket halfway through. 4. Serve the scallops at room temperature or thoroughly chilled after tossing with the remaining ingredients.

Per Serving: Calories 420 ; Fat 37.4 g; Sodium 79 mg; Carbs 2.4g; Fiber 0.4g; Sugar 0.83g; Protein 19.1g

Halibut Hamburgers

Prep time: 5 minutes | Cook time: 15 minutes | Serves: 4

1-pound halibut, chopped
2 garlic cloves, crushed
4 tablespoons scallions, chopped
Sea salt and ground black pepper, to taste

1 teaspoon smoked paprika
A pinch of grated nutmeg
1 tablespoon olive oil
4 hamburger buns

1. Combine all the ingredients in a bowl, excluding the hamburger buns. Four patties made from the mixture should be placed in a frying basket for an Air Fryer that has been lightly greased. 2. Place the AirFryer Basket onto the Baking Pan. AirFry in rack Position 2. 3. Set the Function Dial to AirFry. 4. Set Temperature Dial to 400°F. Then turn the ON/Oven Timer dial to the for 14 minutes to turn on the oven and begin AirFrying. 5. Flipping them over halfway through. 6. Enjoy your meal on hamburger buns!

Per Serving: Calories 369 ; Fat 20.8g; Sodium 303 mg; Carbs 23.5g; Fiber 1.4g; Sugar 3.4g; Protein 20.9g

Coconut Shrimp

Prep time: 5 minutes | Cook time: 10 minutes | Serves: 4

½ cup whole wheat flour
1 cup coconut, shredded
¼ cup buttermilk
2 tablespoons olive oil

2 garlic cloves, crushed
1 tablespoon fresh lemon juice
Sea salt and red pepper flakes, to taste
1½ pounds shrimp, peeled and deveined

1. In a mixing bowl, combine the flour, coconut, buttermilk, olive oil, garlic, lemon juice, salt, and red pepper. 2. Put the battered shrimp in an air fryer cooking basket that has been generously oiled. 3. Place the AirFryer Basket onto the Baking Pan. AirFry in rack Position 2. 4. Set the Function Dial to AirFry. 5. Set Temperature Dial to 400°F. Then turn the ON/Oven Timer dial to 9 minutes to turn on the oven and begin AirFrying, flipping the basket halfway through.

Per Serving: Calories 306; Fat 9.7 g; Sodium 1616 mg; Carbs 15.6g; Fiber 2.5g; Sugar 3.27g; Protein 37.9g

Tuna and Veggie Salad

Prep time: 5 minutes | Cook time: 9 minutes | Serves: 4

1-pound fresh tuna steak
Sea salt and ground black pepper, to taste
2 tablespoons fresh lemon juice
1 small onion, thinly sliced

1 carrot, julienned
2 cups baby spinach
2 tablespoons parsley, roughly chopped

1. Place the tuna in a frying basket for an Air Fryer that has been lightly oiled. 2. Toss the fish with salt and black pepper. 3. Place the AirFryer Basket onto the Baking Pan. AirFry in rack Position 2. 4. Set the Function Dial to AirFry. 5. Set Temperature Dial to 400°F. Then turn the ON/Oven Timer dial to 9 minutes to turn on the oven and begin AirFrying, flipping it over halfway through. 6. Use two forks to roughly chop the tuna, then add the remaining ingredients. Stir to blend, then serve thoroughly cold.

Per Serving: Calories 121 ; Fat 1.2 g; Sodium 305 mg; Carbs 5.3g; Fiber 1.3g; Sugar 2.3 g; Protein 23.1g

Tangy Buttery Sea Scallops

Prep time: 5 minutes | Cook time: 7 minutes | Serves: 4

1-pound sea scallops
2 tablespoons butter, room temperature
2 tablespoons lemon juice

2 garlic cloves, crushed
Salt and fresh ground black pepper to taste
¼ cup dry white wine

1. Toss all ingredients in an Air Fryer cooking basket that has been lightly oiled. 2. Place the AirFryer Basket onto the Baking Pan. AirFry in rack Position 2. Set the Function Dial to AirFry. 3. Set Temperature Dial to 400°F. Then turn the ON/Oven Timer dial to 7 minutes to turn on the oven and begin AirFrying, tossing the basket halfway through.

Per Serving: Calories 234 ; Fat 12.9 g; Sodium 256 mg; Carbs 2.21g; Fiber 0.2g; Sugar 0.82g; Protein 27.8g

Juicy Buttery Lobster Tails

Prep time: 5 minutes | Cook time: 8 minutes | Serves: 4

1-pound lobster tails
4 tablespoons butter, room temperature
2 garlic cloves, minced

Coarse sea salt and freshly cracked black pepper, to taste
4 tablespoons springs onions
1 tablespoon fresh lime juice

1. By cutting through the shell, butterfly the lobster tails before putting them in an Air Fryer basket that has been lightly oiled. 2. Combine all of the remaining ingredients in a mixing basin. 3. Now, cover the top of the lobster meat with ½ of the butter mixture. 4. Place the AirFryer Basket onto the Baking Pan. AirFry in rack Position 2. Set the Function Dial to AirFry. 5. Set Temperature Dial to 380°F. Then turn the ON/Oven Timer dial to 4 minutes to turn on the oven and begin AirFrying, tossing the basket halfway through. 6. Then, cover the top with a second ½ of the butter mixture and cook for an additional 4 minutes.

Per Serving: Calories 199 ; Fat 12.4 g; Sodium 573 mg; Carbs 2.33g; Fiber 0.4g; Sugar 0.8g; Protein 19.3g

Chapter 6 Snacks and Appetizers

Crispy Zucchini Sticks

Prep time: 5 minutes | Cook time: 14 minutes | Serves: 4

2 small zucchinis (about ½ pound)
½ teaspoon garlic granules
¼ teaspoon sea salt
⅛ teaspoon freshly ground black pepper

2 teaspoons arrowroot (or cornstarch)
3 tablespoons chickpea flour
1 tablespoon water
Cooking oil spray (sunflower, safflower, or refined coconut

1. Cut the zucchini into sticks that are 2 inches long and ½ inches wide after trimming the ends. You should have roughly 2 cups of sticks in the end. 2. Combine the zucchini sticks with the flour, arrowroot, garlic granules, salt, and pepper in a medium basin. Good stirring. If you have a rubber spatula, use it to mix once more after adding the water. 3. Oil the air fryer basket and add the zucchini sticks, distributing them as widely as you can. Place the AirFryer Basket onto the Baking Pan. AirFry in rack Position 2. 4. Set the Function Dial to AirFry. 5. Set Temperature Dial to 390°F. Then turn the ON/Oven Timer dial to 7 minutes to turn on the oven and begin AirFrying. 6. Take out the basket, give the zucchini a gentle shake or stir to ensure equal cooking, and reapply oil. Cook for a further 7 minutes, or until crisp on the exterior, beautifully browned, and soft inside. 7. Eat the sticks simply or with the dipping sauce of your choice.

Per Serving: Calories 24 ; Fat 0.37 g; Sodium 148 mg; Carbs 3.9g; Fiber 0.6g; Sugar 0.47g; Protein 1.14g

Crispy Green Tomatoes

Prep time: 8 minutes | Cook time: 15 minutes | Serves: 3-4

¾ cup cornmeal
2 tablespoons chickpea or brown rice flour
1 teaspoon seasoned salt
1 teaspoon onion granules

¼ teaspoon freshly ground black pepper
½ cup nondairy milk, plain and unsweetened
Cooking oil spray (coconut, sunflower, or safflower)
2 large green (unripe) tomatoes, cut into ½-inch rounds

1. Combine the cornmeal, flour, seasoned salt, onion, and pepper in a medium basin and whisk until well combined. Place aside. Set aside the milk in a separate medium bowl. 2. Spray oil on the air fryer basket, then set it aside. 3. Start breading the tomatoes after that: Each tomato slice should be dipped in milk before being lightly breaded with the cornmeal mixture. 4. Now is the time to double-dip if you like your coating thicker! Reintroduce the tomato into the milk and then back into the breading. Apply a thick coating to both sides. 5. Spray the air fryer basket with oil and add the coated slices. Repeat the process, adding just enough tomato slices to make a single layer. (A small amount of overlap is acceptable; just avoid overcrowding the basket to prevent improper browning.) Spray the tops liberally with oil until no dry breading areas are visible. 6. Place the AirFryer Basket onto the Baking Pan. AirFry in rack Position2. 7. Set the Function Dial to AirFry. 8. Set Temperature Dial to 390°F. Then turn the ON/Oven Timer dial to 6 minutes to turn on the oven and begin AirFrying. 9. After 6 minutes, remove the air fryer basket from the pan. 10. Reapply oil to the tops and gently flip each tomato slice over, being careful not to overlap them too much. Spray oil liberally once more until no dry spots are visible. 11. 3 more minutes of frying. With no need to turn them this time, remove the basket and cook the food for an additional 3 to 6 minutes, or until crisp and golden-brown. Take out onto a platter.

Per Serving: Calories 190 ; Fat 1.51g; Sodium 617 mg; Carbs 39.5g; Fiber 3.1g; Sugar 9.8g; Protein 5.2g

Simple Air-Fried Zucchini

Prep time: 5 minutes | Cook time: 14 minutes | Serves: 4

Cooking oil spray (sunflower, safflower, or refined coconut)
2 zucchinis, sliced in ¼- to ½-inch-thick rounds (about 2 cups)
¼ teaspoon garlic granules

⅛ teaspoon sea salt
Freshly ground black pepper (optional)

1. Spray oil on the air fryer basket. Spread out the zucchini rounds as much as you can inside the basket. If used, equally distribute the garlic, salt, and pepper over the tops. 2. Place the AirFryer Basket onto the Baking Pan. AirFry in rack Position 2. Set the Function Dial to AirFry. Set Temperature Dial to 390°F. Then turn the ON/Oven Timer dial to 7 minutes to turn on the oven and begin AirFrying. 3. Take out the air fryer basket, turn the zucchini with a spatula to ensure consistent cooking, and reapply oil. 4. Roast the zucchini rounds for a further 7 minutes, or until well browned and soft.

Per Serving: Calories 2 ; Fat 0.08 g; Sodium 78 mg; Carbs 0.23g; Fiber 0.1g; Sugar 0.13g; Protein 0.07g

Roasted Eggplant with Tamari

Prep time: 5 minutes | Cook time: 13 minutes | Serves: 4

Cooking oil spray (sunflower, safflower, or refined coconut)
1 medium-size eggplant (1 pound), cut into ½-inch-thick slices
2½ tablespoons tamari or shoyu

2 teaspoons garlic granules
2 teaspoons onion granules
4 teaspoons oil (olive, sunflower, or safflower)

1. Spray oil on the air fryer basket, then set it aside. 2. Add the tamari, garlic, onion, and oil to a large bowl with the eggplant pieces. Stir thoroughly, coating the eggplant as uniformly as you can. 3. In the air fryer basket, arrange the eggplant in a single layer (or, ideally, two layers). 4. Place the AirFryer Basket onto the Baking Pan. AirFry in rack Position 2. Set the Function Dial to Air Fry. Set the Temperature Dial to 390°F. Then turn the ON/Oven Timer dial to 5 minutes to turn on the oven and begin air frying. 5. The eggplant should be removed and put back in the bowl. Place the eggplant slices back in the air fryer as before and toss to evenly coat with the remaining liquid mixture. 6. Roast for another 3 minutes. To ensure equal cooking, take the basket out and turn the pieces over. 7. Roast the eggplant for a further 5 minutes, or until it is well browned and extremely soft.

Per Serving: Calories 135 ; Fat 37.4 g; Sodium 79 mg; Carbs 2.4g; Fiber 0.4g; Sugar 0.83g; Protein 19.1g

Carrots with Balsamic Glaze

Prep time: 5 minutes | Cook time: 18 minutes | Serves: 3

3 medium-size carrots (about ⅓ pound)
1 tablespoon orange juice
2 teaspoons balsamic vinegar
1 teaspoon cooking oil (sunflower, avocado, or safflower)

1 teaspoon maple syrup
½ teaspoon dried rosemary
¼ teaspoon sea salt
¼ teaspoon lemon zest

1. There is no need to peel the carrots; simply trim the ends and scrub them. Cut them into 2-inch spears with a 1-inch thickness. 2. Fill the AirFryer Basket with carrots. 3. Add the orange juice, oil, maple syrup, rosemary, balsamic vinegar, salt, and zest. Good stirring. 4. Place the AirFryer Basket onto the Baking Pan. AirFry in rack Position 2. Set the Function Dial to AirFry. Set the Temperature Dial to 390°F. Then turn the ON/Oven Timer dial to 4 minutes to turn on the oven and begin air frying. 5. Stir the mixture thoroughly after removing the pan. Five more minutes of roasting. Cook for an additional five minutes after taking the pan out of the oven. 6. Take out the pan and stir only once more. Cook the carrots for a further 4 minutes, or until they are bright orange, thoroughly glazed (the sauce has thickened and is coating the carrots rather than remaining liquid and thin), and reasonably tender. when still heated.

Per Serving: Calories 50 ; Fat 1.66 g; Sodium 237 mg; Carbs 8.5g; Fiber 1.7g; Sugar 5.1g; Protein 0.6g

Cauliflower Bites with Buffalo Sauce

Prep time: 15 minutes | Cook time: 12 minutes | Serves: 4

For the Cauliflower:
2 cups cauliflower florets (cut into bite-size pieces)
2 tablespoons nondairy milk, plain and unsweetened, plus 2 tablespoons
1 tablespoon ground flaxseed
½ cup chickpea flour
For the Buffalo Sauce:
½ teaspoon arrowroot (or cornstarch)
¼ cup chickpea liquid, divided
¼ cup hot sauce
For Dipping:
No-Dairy Ranch Dressing, or bottled vegan ranch

1 tablespoon arrowroot (or cornstarch)
½ teaspoon garlic granules
½ teaspoon onion granules
⅛ teaspoon baking soda
Cooking oil spray (sunflower, safflower, or refined coconut)

2 large garlic cloves, minced or pressed
2 teaspoons vegan margarine

Preparing the cauliflower: 1. Combine the cauliflower with 2 tablespoons of milk and the flaxseed in a small bowl. Stir and wait five to ten minutes. 2. Blend the flour, arrowroot, garlic, onion, and baking soda in a medium basin and whisk to thoroughly combine. 3. Spray oil into the air fryer basket, then place it aside. While keeping the milk-flax bowl, remove the flaky cauliflower pieces and add them to the flour mixture. Stir thoroughly (though gently) to coat the cauliflower with the mixture using a rubber spatula or a large spoon. 4. The tiny basin will be filled with the final 2 tablespoons of milk after stirring. Reintroduce the floured cauliflower to the liquid and thoroughly stir. Reintroduce the cauliflower to the flour mixture after that. To ensure that the batter covers the cauliflower evenly, stir thoroughly. 5. Stuff the air fryer basket with the cauliflower. Spray some oil on. 6. Place the AirFryer Basket onto the Baking Pan. AirFry in rack Position 2. 7. Set the Function Dial to AirFry. 8. Set Temperature Dial to 390°F. Then turn the ON/Oven Timer dial to 6 minutes to turn on the oven and begin AirFrying ,shake it or stir it to ensure that the cauliflower cooks equally on all sides, then re-spray with oil and fry for an additional six minutes.

Preparing the Buffalo sauce: 1. Stir the arrowroot and a tablespoon of the chickpea liquid together in a small bowl until the arrowroot is completely dissolved. 2. Combine the spicy sauce, arrowroot combination, garlic, and vegan margarine in a medium-sized pot over medium-high heat. Set aside. Cook, whisking or swirling often, for 1 to 2 minutes, or until somewhat thicker in texture. 3. Combine the buffalo sauce with the cauliflower and mix to coat. Put the sauce-coated cauliflower in the baking pan. 4. Set the Function Dial to AirFry. 5. Set Temperature Dial to 390°F. Then turn the ON/Oven Timer dial to the 3-5 minutes to turn on the oven and begin AirFrying. 6. Serve hot with No-Dairy Ranch Dressing after placing in a bowl and topping with any remaining sauce.

Per Serving: Calories 133 ; Fat 4.6 g; Sodium 495 mg; Carbs 18.5g; Fiber 4.2g; Sugar 4.9g; Protein 5.5g

Crispy Kale Chips

Prep time: 10 minutes | Cook time: 10 minutes | Serves: 3

4 cups lightly packed kale, de-stemmed and torn into 2-inch pieces
2 tablespoons apple cider vinegar
1 tablespoon nutritional yeast

1 tablespoon tamari or shoyu
1 tablespoon oil (olive, sunflower, or melted coconut)
2 large garlic cloves, minced or pressed

1. Toss the kale pieces in a large bowl with the apple cider vinegar, nutritional yeast, tamari, oil, and garlic to coat evenly. Transfer to the AirFryer Basket. 2. Place the AirFryer Basket onto the Baking Pan. AirFry in rack Position 2. Set the Function Dial to AirFry. 3. Set Temperature Dial to 320°F. Then turn the ON/Oven Timer dial to 5 minutes to turn on the oven and begin AirFrying. 4. Remove the cooked food from the air fryer and set it aside: (There probably won't be many at this time.) They will be crisp and dried out. Stir gently, then cook for three more minutes. 5. Take out any crunchy, dry pieces and cook the kale for an additional minute or so, if necessary, to dry it all out.

Per Serving: Calories 69 ; Fat 4.79 g; Sodium 480 mg; Carbs 4.1g; Fiber 1.2g; Sugar 0.6g; Protein 2.9g

Crispy Onion Rings

½ medium-large white onion, peeled
½ cup nondairy milk, plain and unsweetened
¾ cup flour (whole-wheat pastry, chickpea, or all-purpose gluten-free)
1 tablespoon arrowroot (or cornstarch)

¾ teaspoon sea salt, divided
¾ teaspoon freshly ground black pepper, divided
¾ teaspoon garlic granules, divided
1 cup bread crumbs
Cooking oil spray (coconut, sunflower, or safflower)

1. Slice the onion thickly into 1- to 4-inch pieces. About one cup of onion slices should be consumed. With a light touch, carefully split the onion slices into rings. 2. Set aside the milk in a shallow basin. 3. Prepare the initial breading. Mix the flour, arrowroot, ¼ teaspoon each of salt, pepper, and garlic in a medium bowl. Stir thoroughly and reserve. 4. The second breading should be made. Combine the breadcrumbs with ½ teaspoon each of salt, garlic, and onion in a separate medium bowl. Stir thoroughly and reserve. 5. Spray oil into the air fryer basket, then place it aside. 6. Get ready to put together! Each onion ring will proceed as follows: One ring is dipped into the milk. Afterward, dunk in the flour mixture. Dip once more into the milk, then back into the flour mixture, coating completely. Once more dip into the milk, then fully coat in the breadcrumb mixture. Placing it in the air fryer basket with care. 7. Continue by gently arranging the remaining onion rings in the air fryer basket without overlapping them too much. Near the end of this procedure, your fingers will become extremely sticky. the positive news You'll get there, and once things get a little sloppy, you can smoosh the coating onto the final bits. 8. After placing all of the onion rings in the air fryer pan, liberally spray the tops with oil spray. 9. Set the Function Dial to AirFry. 8.Set Temperature Dial to 390°F. Then turn the ON/Oven Timer dial to the 4minutes to turn on the oven and begin AirFrying. Then remove the air fryer pan and fry for another 3 minutes. 10. Remove the air fryer pan, then re-oil the onion rings. Then, very gently remove and flip the pieces over to ensure equal cooking. Spray oil liberally once more, then cook for 4 minutes. 11. After being removed, generously coat the onion rings with oil one last time and cook for 3 minutes, or until they are extremely crunchy and browned. Carefully remove and serve with ketchup or your preferred sauce.

Per Serving: Calories 174 ; Fat 1.97 g; Sodium 659mg; Carbs 34.2g; Fiber 4.1g; Sugar 3.9g; Protein 6.6g

Lime-Roasted Shishito Peppers

½ pound shishito peppers
Cooking oil spray (sunflower, safflower, or refined coconut)
1 tablespoon tamari or shoyu

2 teaspoons fresh lime juice
2 large garlic cloves, pressed

1. Clean the shishito peppers, then set them aside. Spray oil on the air fryer basket. Shishitos should be added after being sprayed with oil. 3 minutes for roasting. 2. Mix the tamari, lime juice, and garlic in a medium bowl while the peppers are cooking. Stir, then transfer to the AirFryer Basket. 3. Place the AirFryer Basket onto the Baking Pan. AirFry in rack Position 2. Set the Function Dial to AirFry. 4. Set Temperature Dial to 392°F. Then turn the ON/Oven Timer dial to 4 minutes to turn on the oven and begin AirFrying. Reapply oil to the peppers and roast for three more minutes. 5. After shaking the basket one final time, remove it and mist the peppers with oil. Continue roasting for a further 3 minutes, or until many of them startled you with a popping sound and had many lovely browned spots on them (giving them that well-roasted appearance). 6. Add the shishitos to the tamari mixture in the basin. After uniformly coating the peppers, toss and serve. The peppers are eaten with your hands, and the stems are thrown away as you go. Enjoy your brand-new compulsion!

Per Serving: Calories 50 ; Fat 1.66 g; Sodium 237 mg; Carbs 8.5g; Fiber 1.7g; Sugar 5.1g; Protein 0.6g

Traditional Taro Chips

Prep time: 5 minutes | Cook time: 13 minutes | Serves: 2

Cooking oil spray (coconut, sunflower, or safflower)
1 cup thinly sliced taro

Sea salt

1. Spray oil on the air fryer basket, then set it aside. Spread out the sliced taro as much as you can in the AirFryer Basket before adding the oil. 2. Place the AirFryer Basket onto the Baking Pan. AirFry in rack Position 2. Set the Function Dial to AirFry. 3. Set Temperature Dial to 320°F. Then turn the ON/Oven Timer dial to 4 minutes to turn on the oven and begin AirFrying. 4. Take off the air fryer basket, jiggle it (to ensure that the chips cook equally), and reapply oil. 4 more minutes of frying. Remove any crisp or browned chips at this time. 5. Take out the air fryer basket, give it another shake, give it another spray, and give it a light salting, to taste. Fry for a further three to four minutes. 6. All of the cooked chips should be taken out, and any that are still undercooked should be cooked for one more minute or until crisp. Please keep in mind that they won't all cook at the same rate in the air fryer, so some may require additional time. 7. They may also become somewhat crispier after sitting at room temperature for a few minutes. After making a few batches, you'll be able to test for doneness with ease.

Per Serving: Calories 58 ; Fat 0.1 g; Sodium 6 mg; Carbs 13.7g; Fiber 2.1g; Sugar 0.2g; Protein 0.78g

Lime Tortilla Chips

Prep time: 5 minutes | Cook time: 7 minutes | Serves: 3

4 corn tortillas
½ teaspoon garlic granules
⅛ to ¼ teaspoon sea salt

2½ teaspoons fresh lime juice
Cooking oil spray (coconut, sunflower, or safflower)

1. Divide each tortilla into four halves. Place in a medium bowl and gently toss with the lime juice, garlic, and salt to taste. 2. Spray the oil in the air fryer basket, add the chips. Place the AirFryer Basket onto the Baking Pan. AirFry in rack Position 2. 3. Set Temperature Dial to 350°F. Then turn the ON/Oven Timer dial to 3 minutes to turn on the oven and begin AirFrying. 4. To ensure that the chips cook evenly, remove the air fryer basket, toss, and reapply oil. 2 more minutes of frying. After one final removal, throw the food in oil and fry for two minutes, or until golden and crisp. 5. As you go, make sure to remove the ones that are done because they might not all cook at the same rate. Allow to crisp up completely by sitting at room temperature for a few minutes, and then eat.

Per Serving: Calories72 ; Fat 0.9 g; Sodium 118 mg; Carbs 14.7g; Fiber 2g; Sugar 0.36g; Protein 1.8g

Cheese Stuffed Zucchini Rolls

Prep time: 15 minutes | Cook time: 5 minutes | Serves: 2-4

3 zucchinis, sliced thinly lengthwise with a mandolin or very sharp knife
1 tbsp. olive oil

1 cup goat cheese
¼ tsp. black pepper and salt

1. Lightly brush olive oil onto each zucchini strip. 2. Combine the goat cheese, black pepper, and sea salt. 3. Place a small, equal quantity of goat cheese in the middle of each zucchini strip. The strips are rolled up and fastened with toothpicks. 4. Place in the Air Fryer Basket. Place the AirFryer Basket onto the Baking Pan. AirFry in rack Position 2 and set Temperature Dial to 390°F. Then turn the ON/Oven Timer dial to 5 minutes to turn on the oven and begin AirFrying or until the zucchini is just starting to get crispy. Add additional tomato sauce on top, if desired.

Per Serving: Calories 149 ; Fat 3.55 g; Sodium 309 mg; Carbs 26.25g; Fiber 2.9g; Sugar 1.2g; Protein 3.43g

Sweet Potato Chips with Rosemary

Prep time: 5 minutes | Cook time: 12 minutes | Serves: 2

Cooking oil spray (coconut, sunflower, or safflower)
1 small-medium sweet potato, unpeeled, thinly sliced (about 1 cup)

¼ teaspoon dried rosemary
Dash sea salt

1. Oil the air fryer basket by using a spray bottle. Spread out the sweet potato slices as much as you can inside the basket. Spray oil on the tops. 2. Place the AirFryer Basket onto the Baking Pan. AirFry in rack Position 2. Set Temperature Dial to 390°F. Then turn the ON/Oven Timer dial to 4 minutes to turn on the oven and begin AirFrying. 3. Remove the air fryer pan, reapply the oil, and top the potato slices with the rosemary and sea salt. Repeat the oil spraying and cook for an additional 4 minutes. 4. Take out the air fryer pan, shake it, spritz the pieces with oil, and fry for a further 4 minutes, or until they are just beginning to brown. 5. Due to differing thicknesses, chips may cook at somewhat different speeds; thus, remove any that are cooked before those that require more time. 6. Additionally, they will typically crisp up after being transferred to a platter and left at room temperature for a minute, so if they appear lightly browned, they are most likely done. (It's better to undercook them at this point; if they don't crisp up at room temperature, you can always put them back in the air fryer.) 7. Until all of the pieces are browned, cook the food as before, checking frequently. 8. Once crisp, you can serve and, if you'd like, cook additional batches.

Per Serving: Calories 50 ; Fat 1.66 g; Sodium 237 mg; Carbs 8.5g; Fiber 1.7g; Sugar 5.1g; Protein 0.6g

Traditional French Fries

Prep time: 5 minutes | Cook time: 22 minutes | Serves: 3

2 medium potatoes
Cooking oil spray (sunflower, safflower, or refined coconut)
2 teaspoons oil (olive, sunflower, or melted coconut)
½ teaspoon garlic granules

¼ teaspoon plus ⅛ teaspoon sea salt
¼ teaspoon freshly ground black pepper
¼ teaspoon paprika
Ketchup, hot sauce, or No-Dairy Ranch Dressing, for serving

1. After washing the potatoes, cut them into about uniform-sized French fry shapes that are ¼-inch thick. Spray some oil on the air fryer basket and place it aside. 2. In a medium bowl, combine the oil, garlic, salt, pepper, and paprika with the diced potatoes. Stir thoroughly (I use a rubber spatula). Transfer to the AirFryer Basket. Place the AirFryer Basket onto the Baking Pan. AirFry in rack Position 2. 3. Set Temperature Dial to 390°F. Then turn the ON/Oven Timer dial to 8 minutes to turn on the oven and begin AirFrying. 4. Take out the air fryer basket and give it a gentle swirl. 8 more minutes of frying. Once again remove, mix, and cook for a further 6 minutes, or until the food is soft and well browned. 5. Enjoy with ketchup, spicy sauce, vegan ranch, or any other condiment of your choosing, or simply plain.

Per Serving: Calories 240 ; Fat 3.9 g; Sodium 222 mg; Carbs 46.8g; Fiber 6.3g; Sugar 4.29g; Protein 5.6g

French Fries with Shallots and Cheese

Prep time: 15 minutes | Cook time: 19 minutes | Serves: 3

Cooking oil spray (sunflower, safflower, or refined coconut)
1 large potato (russet or Yukon Gold), cut into ¼-inch-thick slices
1 teaspoon neutral-flavored oil (sunflower, safflower, or refined coconut)

¼ teaspoon sea salt
⅛ teaspoon freshly ground black pepper
1 large shallot, thinly sliced
½ cup plus 2 tablespoons prepared Cheesy Sauce
2 tablespoons minced chives or scallions (optional)

1. Oil the air fryer basket using a spray bottle. Place aside. 2. Combine the oil, salt, and pepper with the potato pieces in a medium bowl. Transfer to the AirFryer Basket. Place the AirFryer Basket onto the Baking Pan. AirFry in rack Position 2. 3. Set Temperature Dial to 390°F. Then turn the ON/Oven Timer dial to 6 minutes to turn on the oven and begin AirFrying .To ensure that the slices cook uniformly, remove the air fryer pan, toss it, and fry for an additional 4 minutes. 4. Remove. Shake the shallots in and cook for an additional five minutes. 5. Follow these instructions to make the cheesy sauce. Place aside or keep heated on a burner with a very low heat. 6. Take the air fryer basket out, shake it or stir it, and fry for a further 4 minutes, or until the fries and shallots are crisp and golden. 7. Serve with Cheesy Sauce on top and, if you'd like, a dash of chives or scallions.

Per Serving: Calories 125 ; Fat 1.7 g; Sodium 507 mg; Carbs23.15g; Fiber 3.7g; Sugar 2.9g; Protein 3.3g

Sweet Brussels Sprouts with Miso Glaze

Prep time: 8 minutes | Cook time: 11 minutes | Serves: 4

Cooking oil spray (sunflower, safflower, or refined coconut)
2½ cups trimmed Brussels sprouts
1½ tablespoons maple syrup
1½ teaspoons mellow white miso
1 teaspoon toasted sesame oil

1 to 1½ teaspoons tamari or shoyu, divided
2 large garlic cloves, pressed or finely minced
1 teaspoon grated fresh ginger
¼ to ½ teaspoon red chili flakes

1. Oil the air fryer basket by using a spray bottle. In the air fryer basket, add the trimmed 2½ cups of Brussels sprouts and coat with oil. 2. Place the AirFryer Basket onto the Baking Pan. AirFry in rack Position 2. Set Temperature Dial to 390°F. Then turn the ON/Oven Timer dial to 6 minutes to turn on the oven and begin AirFrying. Take the air fryer basket out, shake it, and then re-oil the Brussels sprouts. Continue frying for a further 5 minutes, or until they are crisp-tender and thoroughly browned (ideally, they should be a peculiar, glorious mixture of brilliant green with plenty of really browned, roasted patches). 3. Combine the miso and maple syrup in a medium basin. until smooth, whisk. Add the garlic, ginger, sesame oil, 1 teaspoon tamari, and chili flakes. Good stirring. Add the cooked Brussels sprouts to the bowl, along with the sauce, and stir to incorporate. If you want them to taste saltier, you can add the extra half teaspoon of tamari. Serve right away. 4. Brussels sprouts should be prepared by cutting off the base, removing the outer leaves, and then rinsing (unless they look perfect and are free of flaws). 5. Cut them in half if they are particularly big. The main thing is to make sure the pieces are equal in size so that they cook at the same rate. If they are little, leave them as they are.

Per Serving: Calories 62 ; Fat 1.5 g; Sodium 173 mg; Carbs 11.2g; Fiber 2.3g; Sugar 5.9g; Protein 2.3g

Fries with Berbere Spice

1 large (about ¾ pound) potato (preferably Yukon Gold, but any kind will do)
Cooking oil spray (sunflower, safflower, or refined coconut)
1 tablespoon neutral-flavored cooking oil (sunflower, safflower, or refined coconut)
1 teaspoon coconut sugar

1 teaspoon garlic granules
½ teaspoon berbere
½ teaspoon sea salt
¼ teaspoon turmeric
¼ teaspoon paprika

1. After washing the potato, cut it into roughly uniform pieces that resemble French fries and are about ¼-inch thick. Spray some oil on the air fryer basket and place it aside. 2. Combine the potato pieces with the oil, sugar, garlic, berbere, salt, turmeric, and paprika in a medium bowl and well mix (I use a rubber spatula). Transfer to the AirFryer Basket. Place the AirFryer Basket onto the Baking Pan. AirFry in rack Position 2. 3. Set Temperature Dial to 390°F. Then turn the ON/Oven Timer dial to 8 minutes to turn on the oven and begin AirFrying. 4. Take out the air fryer pan and give it a good shake (or gentle swirl). 8 more minutes of frying. 5. Remove off the heat one last time, shake or mix, and cook for an additional 3 to 5 minutes, or until the meat is tender and beautifully browned. Enjoy while it's still warm or hot.

Per Serving: Calories 214 ; Fat 7.3 g; Sodium 593 mg; Carbs 34.4g; Fiber 4.3g; Sugar 2.7g; Protein 3.9g

"Samosas" with Cilantro Chutney

2½ cups diced potato (about 2 medium potatoes), cooked until tender
¼ cup peas
2 teaspoons oil (coconut, sunflower, or safflower)
3 large garlic cloves, minced or pressed
1½ tablespoons fresh lime juice
1½ teaspoons cumin powder
1 teaspoon onion granules

1 teaspoon coriander powder
½ teaspoon sea salt
½ teaspoon turmeric
¼ teaspoon cayenne powder
10 rice paper wrappers, square or round
Cooking oil spray (sunflower, safflower, or refined coconut)
Cilantro Chutney

1. Using a potato masher or a large fork, thoroughly mash the potatoes in a large bowl. Peas, oil, garlic, lime, cumin, onion, coriander, salt, turmeric, and cayenne are to be added. Stir vigorously until everything is well-combined. 2. Pour water into a medium basin or shallow dish. Give a rice paper wrapper a brief soak in the water. Place it on a smooth, clean surface; avoid placing it on wood or any other absorbent materials. The potato filling should be placed in the centre of the wrapper, then rolled up whichever you like. Because I like using circular brown rice wraps, I usually wrap them like a burrito or spring roll. However, you can use square wraps and fold your "samosas" into triangles if you like a more conventional samosa shape. 3. Repeat step 2 as necessary to produce all of the "samosas" you intend to serve right away. 4. Spray the air fryer pan with oil and add some "samosas," putting some space between each one (if they touch each other, they may stick). Spray oil on the tops. 5. Set Temperature Dial to 390°F. Then turn the ON/Oven Timer dial to 9 minutes to turn on the oven and begin AirFrying or until extremely hot and just beginning to turn a little crunchy. Allow it cool for a few (what will feel like an eternity) minutes, then serve with Cilantro Chutney as a dipping sauce.

Per Serving: Calories 205 ; Fat 2.5 g; Sodium 331 mg; Carbs 42.7g; Fiber 2.8g; Sugar 4.2g; Protein 3.6g

Lime Spiced Okra

½ pound okra (3 cups)
1 tablespoon coconut oil, melted
1 teaspoon cumin
1 teaspoon coriander
1 teaspoon garlic granules

¼ teaspoon sea salt
¼ teaspoon turmeric
⅛ teaspoon cayenne
1 teaspoon fresh lime juice

1. In a medium bowl, combine the oil and okra. Salt, turmeric, cayenne, garlic, cumin, and coriander should also be added. Stir thoroughly, preferably with a rubber spatula, so the seasonings are evenly distributed throughout the okra. 2. Place the okra in the air fryer basket onto the Baking Pan. AirFry in rack Position 2. 3. Set Temperature Dial to 390°F. Then turn the ON/Oven Timer dial to the 7 minutes to turn on the oven and begin AirFrying. 4. Discard the seasoning bowl. Return the air fryer pan, stir or toss the okra to ensure equal cooking, and fry for an additional 7 minutes. Take the pan out, toss, and assess the food's doneness. Depending on the size of your okra, you'll likely need to fry it for an additional 6 minutes at this time (smaller pieces cook more quickly). 5. Remove when the pieces are "crumbly" as opposed to "squishy." Smaller pieces of okra may need to be removed if there are different sizes present because they will cook more quickly than larger portions. 6. Return the okra to the seasoning dish once it has all become crunchy. After giving the okra one more stir, squeeze some lime juice over it, and then serve right away.

Per Serving: Calories 52 ; Fat 3.6 g; Sodium 150 mg; Carbs 4.9g; Fiber 2g; Sugar 0.89g; Protein 1.2g

Crispy Cauliflower Pakoras

⅔ cup chickpea flour
1 tablespoon arrowroot (or cornstarch)
1½ teaspoons sea salt
2 teaspoons cumin powder
½ teaspoon coriander powder
½ teaspoon turmeric
⅛ teaspoon baking soda

⅛ teaspoon cayenne powder
1½ cups minced onion
½ cup chopped cilantro
½ cup finely chopped cauliflower
¼ cup fresh lemon juice
Cooking oil spray (coconut, sunflower, or safflower)

1. Chickpea flour, arrowroot, salt, cumin, coriander, turmeric, baking soda, and cayenne are mixed together in a medium bowl. Good stirring. 2. Combine the flour mixture with the onion, cilantro, cauliflower, and lemon juice. Mix thoroughly. Place aside. 3. Spray oil into the air fryer pan, then place it aside. Also take a plate and set it aside. 4. Get your hands filthy for a good cause right now. Restir the mixture while rubbing the flour and spices into the veggies with your hands. Afterward, start forming the pakoras: The goal is to keep the pieces tiny so they will cook completely. Take a tablespoon of the little pieces and combine them in your palm to form a 1-inch ball. Put the item in the air fryer. 5. Repeat the process, forming pakoras with the remaining batter, and arranging them in the basket, being sure to leave space between each one to prevent them from touching. Ultimately, you'll probably divide the mixture in halves and cook half of it later on a plate and the other half in the air fryer basket. Place the AirFryer Basket onto the Baking Pan. AirFry in rack Position 2. 6. Use a good amount of oil to generously coat the tops of the pakoras in the air fryer, Set Temperature Dial to 350°F. Then turn the ON/Oven Timer dial to 4 minutes to turn on the oven and begin AirFrying. Remove the air fryer basket, liberally spray with oil once more, and fry for an additional four minutes. 7. Remove the basket, then re-oil the pakoras. Turn each one over slowly. Spray oil on the tops, then fry for four minutes. Take the basket out, spray the pan with oil liberally once again, and cook the food for a final 4 minutes, or until it is well browned and crisp. Instantaneously serve either simple or with some cilantro chutney. 8. Repeat steps 4 through 7 with the leftover batter, or put it in the refrigerator for later use (the batter will last about 5 days in an airtight container, refrigerated).

Per Serving: Calories 77 ; Fat 1.13 g; Sodium 745 mg; Carbs 13.7g; Fiber 2.4g; Sugar 3.3g; Protein 3.6g

Delicious Spring Rolls

Prep time: 10 minutes | Cook time: 13 minutes | Serves: 16

4 teaspoons toasted sesame oil
6 medium garlic cloves, minced or pressed
1 tablespoon grated fresh ginger
2 cups shiitake mushrooms, thinly sliced
4 cups chopped green cabbage
1 cup grated carrots

½ teaspoon sea salt
16 rice paper wraps
Cooking oil spray (sunflower, safflower, or refined coconut)
Asian Spicy Sweet Sauce or bottled Thai Sweet Chili Sauce (optional)

1. Add the toasted sesame oil, garlic, ginger, mushrooms, cabbage, carrots, and salt to a wok or sauté pan that has been heated over medium heat. When the cabbage is just beginning to wilt, stir often for 3 to 4 minutes. Get rid of the heat. 2. If using rice paper, gently remove a piece from the package, wet it, and then place it on a smooth, non-absorbent surface (such as a granite countertop). In the centre, distribute roughly ¼ cup of the filling. Fold the bottom up over the filling once the wrapper is flexible enough to roll; then, fold the sides in. Next, completely roll up. Make a little burrito, in essence. 3. Continue doing this until you have as many spring rolls as you want to consume at this moment (and the amount that will fit in the air fryer basket without any of them touching each other). 4. Spray the air fryer basket with oil and add the spring rolls, leaving some space between them to prevent sticking. Spray oil on the top of each spring roll. Place the AirFryer Basket onto the Baking Pan. AirFry in rack Position 2, then Set Temperature Dial to 390°F. Then turn the ON/Oven Timer dial to 9 minutes to turn on the oven and begin AirFrying or until the tops are just beginning to crisp and brown. 5. Serve right away either plain or with sauce. The remaining filling will last for about a week in the refrigerator (in an airtight container).

Per Serving: Calories 70 ; Fat 1.38 g; Sodium 128 mg; Carbs 13.3g; Fiber 1g; Sugar 1.32g; Protein 1.22g

Garlicky Potatoes

Prep time: 15 minutes | Cook time: 30 minutes | Serves: 4

1 lb. russet baking potatoes
1 tbsp. garlic powder
1 tbsp. freshly chopped parsley

½ tsp. salt
¼ tsp. black pepper
1 – 2 tbsps. olive oil

1. After washing the potatoes, dry them using fresh paper towels. 2. Use a fork to pierce each potato many times. 3. Add the salt, pepper, and garlic powder to a large bowl with the potatoes. 4. Add the olive oil and stir well. 5. Transfer to the AirFryer Basket. Place the AirFryer Basket onto the Baking Pan. AirFry in rack Position 2, then Set Temperature Dial to 360°F. Then turn the ON/Oven Timer dial to 30 minutes to turn on the oven and begin AirFrying , shaking the basket occasionally. 6. Serve the potatoes with butter, sour cream, or another dipping sauce, if desired, and top with the parsley that has been finely chopped.

Per Serving: Calories 149 ; Fat 3.5 g; Sodium 309 mg; Carbs 26.25g; Fiber 2.9g; Sugar 1.2g; Protein 3.43g

Garlic Asparagus

Prep time: 15 minutes | Cook time: 10 minutes | Serves: 4

10 asparagus spears, woody end cut off
1 clove garlic, minced
4 tbsp. olive oil

Pepper to taste
Salt to taste

1. Combine the oil and garlic in a bowl. 2. Place the asparagus in the fryer basket and cover with this mixture. Salt and pepper should be added. 3. Place the AirFryer Basket onto the Baking Pan. AirFry in rack Position 2. 4. Set the Function Dial to AirFry. 5. Set Temperature Dial to 400°F. Then turn the ON/Oven Timer dial to 10 minutes to turn on the oven and begin AirFrying. 6. After 10 minutes of cooking, serve hot.

Per Serving: Calories 130 ; Fat 13.7 g; Sodium 1 mg; Carbs 1.66g; Fiber 0.4 g; Sugar 0.75g; Protein 0.4g

Cheese Zucchini Chips

Prep time: 15 minutes | Cook time: 25 minutes | Serves: 2

3 medium zucchini, sliced
1 tsp. parsley, chopped
3 tbsps. parmesan cheese, grated

Pepper to taste
Salt to taste

1. Spray cooking spray on a piece of baking paper, then arrange the sliced zucchini on it. 2. Cheese, pepper, parsley, and salt should all be combined. Sprinkle the zucchini with this mixture. 3. Place the zucchini slices in the Air Fryer and Place the AirFryer Basket onto the Baking Pan. AirFry in rack Position 2. 4. Set the Function Dial to AirFry. 5. Set Temperature Dial to 425°F. Then turn the ON/Oven Timer dial to 25 minutes to turn on the oven and begin AirFrying. Making sure the slices are properly browned before serving.

Per Serving: Calories 50 ; Fat 2.8 g; Sodium 138 mg; Carbs 3.75 g; Fiber 0.5 g; Sugar 1.17g; Protein 3.05g

Spicy Sweet Potatoes Wedges

Prep time: 15 minutes | Cook time: 20 minutes | Serves: 2

2 large sweet potatoes, cut into wedges
1 tbsp. olive oil
1 tsp. chili powder
1 tsp. mustard powder

1 tsp. cumin
1 tbsp. Mexican seasoning
Pepper to taste
Salt to taste

1. Combine all of the ingredients in a bowl to thoroughly coat the sweet potatoes. 2. After placing the wedges in the Air Fryer basket, place the AirFryer Basket onto the Baking Pan. AirFry in rack Position 2. 3. Set the Function Dial to AirFry. 4. Set Temperature Dial to 350°F. Then turn the ON/Oven Timer dial to 20 minutes to turn on the oven and begin AirFrying, shake it every five minutes for the duration of the 20 minutes.

Per Serving: Calories 50 ; Fat 2.8 g; Sodium 138 mg; Carbs 3.75 g; Fiber 0.5 g; Sugar 1.17g; Protein 3.05g

Cajun Potato Wedges

Prep time: 15 minutes | Cook time: 20 minutes | Serves: 4

4 medium potatoes, cut into wedges
1 tbsp. Cajun spice
1 tbsp. olive oil

Pepper to taste
Salt to taste

1. After placing the wedges in the Air Fryer basket, Place the AirFryer Basket onto the Baking Pan. AirFry in rack Position 2. 2. Set the Function Dial to AirFry. 3. Set Temperature Dial to 370°F. Then turn the ON/Oven Timer dial to 20 minutes to turn on the oven and begin AirFrying. 4. Place the fried wedges in a basin and season them with salt, pepper, and Cajun seasoning. Serve hot.

Per Serving: Calories 326; Fat 4.2g; Sodium 24 mg; Carbs 66.4 g; Fiber 8.9 g; Sugar 3.63g; Protein 7.9g

Spicy Bananas Chips

Prep time: 15 minutes | Cook time: 15 minutes | Serves: 3

2 large raw bananas, peel and sliced
½ tsp. red chili powder
1 tsp. olive oil

¼ tsp. turmeric powder
1 tsp. salt

1. Combine some salt and the turmeric powder in a bowl. Place the banana slices in a bowl and sprinkle with salt, chili powder, and olive oil. 2. Put the banana slices in the bowl and give them 10 minutes to soak. 3. After emptying the contents into a sieve, dry the banana slices with a paper towel. Transfer to the AirFryer Basket. 4. Place the AirFryer Basket onto the Baking Pan. AirFry in rack Position 2. 5. Set the Function Dial to AirFry. Set Temperature Dial to 350°F. Then turn the ON/Oven Timer dial to 15 minutes to turn on the oven and begin AirFrying. Once done, serve.

Per Serving: Calories 96 ; Fat 1.8 g; Sodium 790 mg; Carbs 21.1 g; Fiber 1.8 g; Sugar 11.13 g; Protein 1.05g

Sweetened Carrots

Prep time: 15 minutes | Cook time: 20 minutes | Serves: 4

1 tbsp. honey
3 cups baby carrots or carrots, cut into bite-size pieces
1 tbsp. olive oil

Sea salt to taste
Ground black pepper to taste

1. Coat the carrots completely with the olive oil, honey, and carrots in a bowl. 2. Add some salt and freshly ground black pepper. 3. Add the carrots to the Air Fryer Basket. 4. Place the AirFryer Basket onto the Baking Pan. AirFry in rack Position 2. 5. Set the Function Dial to AirFry. 6. Set Temperature Dial to 390°F. Then turn the ON/Oven Timer dial to 12 minutes to turn on the oven and begin AirFrying.

Per Serving: Calories 53; Fat 3.4 g; Sodium 7 mg; Carbs 6.01 g; Fiber 0.4 g; Sugar 5.24 g; Protein 0.29 g

Chapter 7 Desserts

Muffins with Coconut

Prep time: 05 minutes | Cook time: 25 minutes | Serves: 5

½ cup coconut flour
2 tablespoons cocoa powder
3 tablespoons Erythritol
1 teaspoon baking powder

2 tablespoons coconut oil
2 eggs, beaten
½ cup coconut shred

1. Combine all the ingredients in a mixing basin. 2. After that, pour the mixture into the muffin moulds and place them in the baking pan. Fit the baking pan into rack position 2. 3. Set the Function Dial to Bake. Set the Temperature Dial to 350°F. Then turn the ON/Oven Timer dial to 25 minutes to turn on the oven and begin baking.

Per Serving: Calories 114 ; Fat 9.68 g; Sodium 93 mg; Carbs 4.52 g; Fiber 1.2 g; Sugar 1.55g; Protein 4.32g

Espresso Muffins

Prep time: 10 minutes | Cook time: 11 minutes | Serves: 6

1 cup coconut flour
4 tablespoons coconut oil
1 teaspoon vanilla extract
1 teaspoon instant coffee

1 teaspoon baking powder
1 egg, beaten
¼ cup Erythritol

1. Combine the coconut oil, baking powder, egg, erythritol, vanilla extract, and instant coffee in a bowl with the coconut flour. 2. Fill the muffin tins with the mixture, and place them in the baking pan. Fit the baking pan into rack position 2. 3. Set the Function Dial to Bake. Set the Temperature Dial to 375°F. Then turn the ON/Oven Timer dial to 11 minutes to turn on the oven and begin baking.

Per Serving: Calories 111 ; Fat 10.7 g; Sodium 60 mg; Carbs 2.26 g; Fiber 0.5 g; Sugar 1.24g; Protein 1.8g

Cookies with Almonds

Prep time: 05 minutes | Cook time: 15 minutes | Serves: 8

1 cup almond flour
2 oz. almonds, grinded
2 tablespoons Erythritol

½ teaspoon baking powder
5 tablespoons coconut oil, softened
½ teaspoon vanilla extract

1. Combine almonds, erythritol, baking powder, coconut oil, and vanilla extract with the almond flour. Work the dough. 2. Prepare the tiny cookies and put them in the baking pan. Fit the baking pan into rack position 2. 3. Set the Function Dial to Bake. Set the Temperature Dial to 350°F. Then turn the ON/Oven Timer dial to 15 minutes to turn on the oven and begin baking.

Per Serving: Calories 116 ; Fat 12.1 g; Sodium 0 mg; Carbs 1.74 g; Fiber 0.9 g; Sugar 0.35g; Protein 1.53g

Coconut Almond Cookies

2 teaspoons coconut oil, softened
1 tablespoon Erythritol
1 egg, beaten

½ cup coconut flour
1 oz. almonds, chopped

1. In a mixing dish, combine all the ingredients. Work the dough. 2. After that, use the batter to bake cookies and place them in the baking pan. Fit the baking pan into rack position 2.. 3. Set the Function Dial to Bake. Set the Temperature Dial to 365°F. Then turn the ON/Oven Timer dial to 9 minutes to turn on the oven and begin baking.

Per Serving: Calories 66 ; Fat 5.51 g; Sodium 38 mg; Carbs 1.93 g; Fiber 0.8 g; Sugar 0.84g; Protein 2.64g

Homemade Pecan Bars

2 cups coconut flour
5 tablespoons Erythritol
4 tablespoons coconut oil, softened

½ cup heavy cream
1 egg, beaten
4 pecans, chopped

1. Combine the egg, heavy cream, coconut oil, erythritol, and coconut flour. 2. Add the batter to the baking pan and evenly spread it out. 3. Sprinkle pecans on top of the mixture. Fit the baking pan into rack position 2. 4.Set the Function Dial to Bake. Set the Temperature Dial to 350°F. Then turn the ON/Oven Timer dial to 40 minutes to turn on the oven and begin baking. 5. Slice the cooked food into bars.

Per Serving: Calories 326 ; Fat 33.2 g; Sodium 52 mg; Carbs 6.74 g; Fiber 3.9 g; Sugar 2.68g; Protein 4.47g

Dark Muffins

1 egg, beaten
1 tablespoon coconut oil, softened
2 tablespoons almond flour

1 tablespoon cocoa powder
1 tablespoon Erythritol
1 teaspoon ground cinnamon

1. Combine the egg with the coconut oil, almond flour, cocoa, erythritol, and cinnamon powder. 2. Fill the muffin tins with the batter. Transfer to the baking pan. Fit the baking pan into rack position 2. 3.Set the Function Dial to Bake. Set the Temperature Dial to 375°F. Then turn the ON/Oven Timer dial to 10 minutes to turn on the oven and begin baking.

Per Serving: Calories 139 ; Fat 12.5 g; Sodium 52 mg; Carbs 3.39 g; Fiber 1.5 g; Sugar 0.45g; Protein 5.2g

Citrus Coconut Bars

Prep time: 10 minutes | Cook time: 35 minutes | Serves: 10

3 tablespoons coconut oil, melted
3 tablespoons Splenda
1½ cups coconut flour

3 eggs, beaten
1 teaspoon lime zest, grated
3 tablespoons lime juice

1. Place baking paper on the baking pan's bottom.2. Next, combine Splenda with coconut flour, coconut oil, eggs, lime juice, and zest in a mixing bowl. 3. Add the mixture to the baking pan and gently press it down. Fit the baking pan into rack position 2. 4. Set the Function Dial to Bake. Set the Temperature Dial to 350°F. Then turn the ON/Oven Timer dial to 35 minutes to turn on the oven and begin baking. 5. After a brief period of cooling, cut the prepared food into bars.

Per Serving: Calories 82; Fat7.05 g; Sodium 69 mg; Carbs 2.06 g; Fiber 0.4 g; Sugar 1.22 g; Protein 2.97g

Delicious Macadamia Nut Bars

Prep time: 15 minutes | Cook time: 30 minutes | Serves: 10

3 tablespoons butter, softened
1 teaspoon baking powder
1 teaspoon apple cider vinegar
1½ cups coconut flour
3 tablespoons swerve

1 teaspoon vanilla extract
2 eggs, beaten
2 oz. macadamia nuts, chopped
Cooking spray

1. Cooking spray the baking pan first. 2. After that, combine all of the additional ingredients in the mixing bowl and whisk until the mixture is homogeneous. 3. Fill the baking pan with the mixture, fit the baking pan into rack position 2 and set the Function Dial to Bake. Set the Temperature Dial to 350°F. Then turn the ON/Oven Timer dial to 30 minutes to turn on the oven and begin baking. 5. After the mixture has finished cooking, slice it into bars and place them on serving plates.

Per Serving: Calories 106 ; Fat 9.7 g; Sodium 86 mg; Carbs 2.6 g; Fiber 0.9 g; Sugar 1.45g; Protein 2.5g

Coconut Zucchini Bread

Prep time: 10 minutes | Cook time: 40 minutes | Serves: 12

2 cups coconut flour
2 teaspoons baking powder
¾ cup Erythritol
½ cup coconut oil, melted
1 teaspoon apple cider vinegar

1 teaspoon vanilla extract
3 eggs, beaten
1 zucchini, grated
1 teaspoon ground cinnamon

1. Combine baking powder, erythritol, coconut oil, apple cider vinegar, vanilla extract, eggs, zucchini, and ground cinnamon in a bowl with the coconut flour. 2. Spread the ingredients out into the shape of bread in the baking pan. Fit the baking pan into rack position 2 and set the Function Dial to Bake. Set the Temperature Dial to 350°F. Then turn the ON/Oven Timer dial to 40 minutes to turn on the oven and begin baking.

Per Serving: Calories 121 ; Fat 11.5 g; Sodium 68 mg; Carbs 2.38 g; Fiber 0.6 g; Sugar 1.2g; Protein 2.5g

Muffin with Poppy Seeds

Prep time: 10 minutes | Cook time: 10 minutes | Serves: 5

5 tablespoons coconut oil, softened
1 egg, beaten
1 teaspoon vanilla extract
1 tablespoon poppy seeds

1 teaspoon baking powder
2 tablespoons Erythritol
1 cup coconut flour

1. Combine coconut oil, egg, vanilla extract, poppy seeds, baking powder, erythritol, and coconut flour in a large mixing bowl. 2. Spoon the mixture into the muffin moulds once it is homogeneous, then place the moulds in the baking pan. Fit the baking pan into rack position 2. Set the Function Dial to Bake. Set the Temperature Dial to 365°F. Then turn the ON/Oven Timer dial to the 10 minutes to turn on the oven and begin baking.

.**Per Serving:** Calories 165 ; Fat 16.3 g; Sodium 72 mg; Carbs 3.05 g; Fiber 0.9 g; Sugar 1.54g; Protein 2.4g

Lime Almond Pie

Prep time: 10 minutes | Cook time: 35 minutes | Serves: 8

2 eggs, beaten
¾ cup Erythritol
¼ cup almond flour
2 tablespoons coconut oil, melted
1 teaspoon lime zest, grated

1 teaspoon baking powder
1 teaspoon vanilla extract
½ teaspoon apple cider vinegar
1 oz. almonds, chopped

1. In a mixing basin, combine all the ingredients and whisk to a smooth mixture. 2. After that, gently press the mixture into the baking pan. 3. Fit the baking pan into rack position 2. Set the Function Dial to Bake. Set the Temperature Dial to 365°F. Then turn the ON/Oven Timer dial to 35 minutes to turn on the oven and begin baking.

.**Per Serving:** Calories 85 ; Fat 7.6 g; Sodium 26 mg; Carbs 1.48 g; Fiber 0.5 g; Sugar 0.43g; Protein 3g

Flavored Scones

Prep time: 20 minutes | Cook time: 10 minutes | Serves: 6

4 oz. coconut flour
½ teaspoon baking powder
1 teaspoon apple cider vinegar
2 teaspoons mascarpone

¼ cup heavy cream
1 teaspoon vanilla extract
1 tablespoon Erythritol
Cooking spray

1. Combine the coconut flour, baking powder, apple cider vinegar, heavy cream, cheese, vanilla extract, and erythritol in a large mixing bowl. 2. Knead the dough before scones are cut out. 3. After that, put them in the baking pan with cooking spray on them. Fit the baking pan into rack position 2. 3. Set the Function Dial to Bake. Set the Temperature Dial to 365°F. Then turn the ON/Oven Timer dial to 10 minutes to turn on the oven and begin baking.

Per Serving: Calories 29 ; Fat 2.4 g; Sodium 30 mg; Carbs 1.29 g; Fiber 0.2 g; Sugar 0.86g; Protein 0.36g

Lime Raspberries Tart

Prep time: 5 minutes | Cook time: 20 minutes | Serves: 8

5 egg whites
⅓ cup Erythritol
1½ cups coconut flour
1 teaspoon lime zest, grated

1 teaspoon baking powder
⅓ cup coconut oil, melted
3 oz. raspberries
Cooking spray

1. Combine baking powder, coconut oil, coconut flour, erythritol, and lime zest in an egg mixture. 2. Smooth up the mixture by whisking it. 3. After that, pour the batter into the baking pan that has been coated with cooking spray. 4. Place raspberries on top of the batter. Fit the baking pan into rack position 2. Set the Function Dial to Bake. Set the Temperature Dial to 360°F. Then turn the ON/Oven Timer dial to 20 minutes to turn on the oven and begin baking.

Per Serving: Calories 107 ; Fat 9.13 g; Sodium 82 mg; Carbs 4.36 g; Fiber 0.8 g; Sugar 3.47g; Protein 2.66g

Coconut Vanilla Pie

Prep time: 10 minutes | Cook time: 40 minutes | Serves: 8

½ cup coconut cream
3 eggs, beaten
1 tablespoon vanilla extract
1 teaspoon baking powder

3 tablespoons swerve
1 cup coconut flour
1 tablespoon coconut oil, melted

1. Combine coconut flour, coconut oil, swerve, baking powder, and coconut cream with the other ingredients. 2. Next, put the mixture in the baking pan and gently press it down. Fit the baking pan into rack position 2. 3. Set the Function Dial to Bake. Set the Temperature Dial to 355°F. Then turn the ON/Oven Timer dial to 40 minutes to turn on the oven and begin baking.

Per Serving: Calories 124 ; Fat 10.5 g; Sodium 71 mg; Carbs 2.99 g; Fiber 0.7 g; Sugar 1.23g; Protein 4.12g

Donuts with Almonds

Prep time: 15 minutes | Cook time: 7 minutes | Serves: 6

8 ounces almond flour
2 tablespoons Erythritol
1 egg, beaten

2 tablespoons almond butter, softened
4 ounces heavy cream
1 teaspoon baking powder

1. Combine almond flour, erythritol, egg, almond butter, heavy cream, and baking powder in a mixing dish. Work the dough. 2. Using the cutter, roll up the dough and cut out the donuts. 3. Place the doughnuts in the air fryer basket and Place the AirFryer Basket onto the Baking Pan. AirFry in rack Position 2. Set the Function Dial to AirFry. Set Temperature Dial to 365°F. Then turn the ON/Oven Timer dial to 7 minutes to turn on the oven and begin AirFrying.

Per Serving: Calories 340 ; Fat 31.31 g; Sodium 55 mg; Carbs 8.8 g; Fiber 4.7 g; Sugar 2.28g; Protein 9.9g

Spiced Donuts

Prep time: 20 minutes | Cook time: 3 minutes | Serves: 4

1 teaspoon ground nutmeg
½ teaspoon baking powder
½ cup almond flour
1 tablespoon Swerve

1 egg, beaten
1 tablespoon coconut oil, softened
Cooking spray

1. From the inside, spray cooking spray onto the air fryer basket. 2. Next, combine the last few ingredients and knead the dough. 3. Prepare the dough to make the donuts, then air fry them. Place the AirFryer Basket onto the Baking Pan. AirFry in rack Position 2. Set the Function Dial to AirFry. Set Temperature Dial to 390°F. Then turn the ON/Oven Timer dial to 3 minutes to turn on the oven and begin AirFrying.

Per Serving: Calories 44; Fat 4.1 g; Sodium 17 mg; Carbs 0.58 g; Fiber 0.1 g; Sugar 0.12g; Protein 1.5g

Turmeric Coconut Cookies

Prep time: 10 minutes | Cook time: 20 minutes | Serves: 12

2 eggs, beaten
1 tablespoon coconut cream
3 tablespoons coconut oil, melted
2 teaspoons ground turmeric

1 teaspoon vanilla extract
2½ cups coconut flour
2 tablespoons Erythritol

1. In a mixing dish, combine all the ingredients. 2. Knead the dough and use the cutter to make the cookies. 3. Place the cookies in the baking pan. Fit the baking pan into rack position 2 and Set the Function Dial to Bake. Set the Temperature Dial to 350°F. Then turn the ON/Oven Timer dial to 20 minutes to turn on the oven and begin baking.

Per Serving: Calories 44; Fat 4.1 g; Sodium 17 mg; Carbs 0.58 g; Fiber 0.1 g; Sugar 0.12g; Protein 1.5g

Tasty Mint Pie

Prep time: 15 minutes | Cook time: 25 minutes | Serves: 2

1 tablespoon instant coffee
2 tablespoons almond butter, softened
2 tablespoons Erythritol
1 teaspoon dried mint

3 eggs, beaten
1 teaspoon spearmint, dried
4 teaspoons coconut flour
Cooking spray

1. Cooking spray the air fryer basket first. 2. Next, incorporate each ingredient into the mixing bowl. 3. Place the mixture in the baking pan once it is smooth. Gently press it flat. Fit the baking pan into rack position 2. Set the Function Dial to Bake. Set the Temperature Dial to 365°F. Then turn the ON/Oven Timer dial to 25 minutes to turn on the oven and begin baking.

Per Serving: Calories 302; Fat 23.51 g; Sodium 202 mg; Carbs 6.28 g; Fiber 1.9 g; Sugar 2.24g; Protein 17.5g

Cookies with Saffron

Prep time: 10 minutes | Cook time: 15 minutes | Serves: 12

2 cups coconut flour
½ cup Erythritol
¼ cup coconut, melted

1 egg, beaten
2 teaspoons saffron
1 teaspoon vanilla extract

1. In a bowl, combine all the ingredients and knead the dough. 2. After making the cookies, arrange them in a single layer in the baking pan. Fit the baking pan into rack position 2. Set the Function Dial to Bake. Set the Temperature Dial to 355°F. Then turn the ON/Oven Timer dial to 15 minutes to turn on the oven and begin baking.

Per Serving: Calories 21; Fat 0.9 g; Sodium 56 mg; Carbs 1.87 g; Fiber 0.5 g; Sugar 1.27 g; Protein 1.08g

Coconut Cheese Balls

Prep time: 15 minutes | Cook time: 4 minutes | Serves: 10

2 eggs, beaten
1 teaspoon coconut oil, melted
9 oz. coconut flour
5 oz. provolone cheese, shredded

2 tablespoons Erythritol
1 teaspoon baking powder
¼ teaspoon ground coriander
Cooking spray

1. Combine eggs, erythritol, baking powder, cinnamon, Provolone cheese, coconut oil, and coconut flour in a bowl. 2. Create the balls and place them in the baking pan. Fit the baking pan into rack position 2. Set the Function Dial to Bake. Set the Temperature Dial to 400°F. Then turn the ON/Oven Timer dial to 4 minutes to turn on the oven and begin baking.

Per Serving: Calories 85; Fat 6.2 g; Sodium 172 mg; Carbs 1.6 g; Fiber 0.3 g; Sugar 0.88g; Protein 5.61g

Almond Sage Muffins

Prep time: 10 minutes | Cook time: 20 minutes | Serves: 8

3 tablespoons coconut oil, softened
1 egg, beaten
½ cup Erythritol
¼ cup almond flour

1 teaspoon dried sage
3 tablespoons mascarpone
½ teaspoon baking soda
Cooking spray

1. Cooking spray should be used on the muffin tins. 2. After that, combine everything in the mixing bowl and stir until it is smooth. 3. Fill the muffin tins with the mixture, and then place them in the baking pan. 4. Fit the baking pan into rack position 2. Set the Function Dial to Bake. Set the Temperature Dial to 350°F. Then turn the ON/Oven Timer dial to 20 minutes to turn on the oven and begin baking.

Per Serving: Calories 77; Fat 7.94g; Sodium 116 mg; Carbs 0.38 g; Fiber 0 g; Sugar 0.28g; Protein 1.5g

Nut Tarts

Prep time: 10 minutes | Cook time: 10 minutes | Serves: 5

3 pecans, chopped
½ cup coconut flour
1 egg, beaten
1 tablespoon coconut oil, softened

1 tablespoon swerve
½ teaspoon baking powder
Cooking spray

1. Cooking spray the air fryer basket first. 2. Next, combine the egg, coconut oil, swerve, and baking powder with the coconut flour. 3. Once the batter is smooth, pour it into the baking pan, gently press it down, and sprinkle pecans on top. 4. Fit the baking pan into rack position 2. Set the Function Dial to Bake. 5. Set the Temperature Dial to 375°F. Then turn the ON/Oven Timer dial to 10 minutes to turn on the oven and begin baking.

Per Serving: Calories 507; Fat 51.8 g; Sodium 46 mg; Carbs 10.4 g; Fiber 6.6 g; Sugar 3.35 g; Protein 7.9g

Lime Raspberry Jam

Prep time: 10 minutes | Cook time: 20 minutes | Serves: 12

¼ cup Erythritol
7 oz. raspberries

1 tablespoon lime juice
¼ cup of water

1. Fill the air fryer with all the ingredients and gently mix. 2. Place the AirFryer Basket onto the Baking Pan. AirFry in rack Position 2. 3. Set the Function Dial to AirFry. Set Temperature Dial to 350°F. Then turn the ON/Oven Timer dial to 20 minutes to turn on the oven and begin AirFrying.

Per Serving: Calories 15; Fat 0.02 g; Sodium 1 mg; Carbs 3.9 g; Fiber 0.6 g; Sugar 3.34g; Protein 0.14g

Almond Vanilla Shortcake

Prep time: 15 minutes | Cook time: 30 minutes | Serves: 4

3 eggs, beaten
½ cup almond flour
½ teaspoon baking powder
2 teaspoons swerve

1 teaspoon vanilla extract
½ cup coconut cream
Cooking spray

1. Cooking spray the air fryer basket first. 2. Next, combine coconut cream, almond flour, baking powder, swerve, and vanilla essence with the eggs. 3. Pour the smoothed-out mixture into the baking pan and use the spatula to gently press it flat. 4. Fit the baking pan into rack position 2. Set the Function Dial to Bake. 5. Set the Temperature Dial to 355°F. Then turn the ON/Oven Timer dial to 30 minutes to turn on the oven and begin baking.

Per Serving: Calories 201; Fat 17.7 g; Sodium 79 mg; Carbs 3.23 g; Fiber 0.7 g; Sugar 0.63g; Protein 7.85g

Cinnamon Raspberry Cream

Prep time: 10 minutes | Cook time: 20 minutes | Serves: 6

½ cup raspberries
1 tablespoon lime juice
2 tablespoons water

3 tablespoons Erythritol
¼ teaspoon ground cinnamon

1. Blend the raspberries and combine with water, erythritol, lime juice, and crushed cinnamon. 2. Fill the baking pan with the mixture. 3. Fit the baking pan into rack position 2. Set the Function Dial to Bake. 5. Set the Temperature Dial to 345°F. Then turn the ON/Oven Timer dial to the 20 minutes to turn on the oven and begin baking.

Per Serving: Calories 20; Fat 0.03 g; Sodium 1 mg; Carbs 5.29 g; Fiber 0.8 g; Sugar 4.32g; Protein 0.19g

Hand Pies with Coconut

Prep time: 20 minutes | Cook time: 26 minutes | Serves: 6

8 oz. coconut flour
1 teaspoon vanilla extract
2 tablespoons Swerve
2 eggs, beaten

1 tablespoon almond butter, melted
1 tablespoon almond meal
2 tablespoons coconut shred
Cooking spray

1. Combine coconut flour, almond meal, almond butter, swerve, vanilla essence, and eggs. 2. Roll the dough up after kneading it. 3. Cut the dough into squares and top with shredded coconut. 4. Form the squares into pies and place them in the baking pan. 5. Fit the baking pan into rack position 2. Set the Function Dial to Bake. 5. Set the Temperature Dial to 345°F. Then turn the ON/Oven Timer dial to 26 minutes to turn on the oven and begin baking. Flipping halfway through.

Per Serving: Calories 71; Fat 4.9 g; Sodium 85 mg; Carbs 2.5 g; Fiber 0.8 g; Sugar 1.6 g; Protein 3.9g

Coconut Almond milk pie

Prep time: 10 minutes | Cook time: 20 minutes | Serves: 8

2 egg, beaten
3 tablespoons Erythritol
3 tablespoons butter, melted

¼ cup organic almond milk
4 tablespoons coconut flour
½ teaspoon baking powder

1. Combine all ingredients in a mixer bowl and blend until thoroughly combined. 2. Spoon the mixture into the baking pan. Fit the baking pan into rack position 2 and set the Function Dial to Bake. 3. Set the Temperature Dial to 365°F. Then turn the ON/Oven Timer dial to 20 minutes to turn on the oven and begin baking.

Per Serving: Calories 71; Fat 4.9 g; Sodium 85 mg; Carbs 2.5 g; Fiber 0.8 g; Sugar 1.6 g; Protein 3.9g

Keto Almond Vanilla Hot Chocolate

Prep time: 10 minutes | Cook time: 7 minutes | Serves: 3

¼ teaspoon vanilla extract
2 cups organic almond milk
1 teaspoon coconut oil

1 tablespoon cocoa powder
2 tablespoons Erythritol

1. Combine all ingredients in the baking pan. Fit the baking pan into rack position 2. 2. Be sure to smooth out the mixture. Set the Function Dial to Bake. 3. Set the Temperature Dial to 375°F. Then turn the ON/Oven Timer dial to 7 minutes to turn on the oven and begin baking.
.

Per Serving: Calories 98; Fat 3.7 g; Sodium 114 mg; Carbs 16.1 g; Fiber 1.2 g; Sugar 14.08 g; Protein 1.33g

Conclusion

The Cuisinart Air Fryer Toaster Oven is a versatile appliance that can be used for a variety of cooking tasks. While it functions primarily as an air fryer, it can also be used as a toaster oven, increasing its versatility. The Air Fryer Toaster Oven also has a number of features that make it user-friendly, such as a digital display and easy-to-use controls. Overall, the Cuisinart Air Fryer Toaster Oven is a great option for everyone looking for an appliance that can do more than just one thing.

Appendix 1 Measurement Conversion Chart

VOLUME EQUIVALENTS (LIQUID)

US STANDARD	US STANDARD (OUNCES)	METRIC (APPROXIMATE)
2 tablespoons	1 fl.oz	30 mL
¼ cup	2 fl.oz	60 mL
½ cup	4 fl.oz	120 mL
1 cup	8 fl.oz	240 mL
1½ cup	12 fl.oz	355 mL
2 cups or 1 pint	16 fl.oz	475 mL
4 cups or 1 quart	32 fl.oz	1 L
1 gallon	128 fl.oz	4 L

VOLUME EQUIVALENTS (DRY)

US STANDARD	METRIC (APPROXIMATE)
⅛ teaspoon	0.5 mL
¼ teaspoon	1 mL
½ teaspoon	2 mL
¾ teaspoon	4 mL
1 teaspoon	5 mL
1 tablespoon	15 mL
¼ cup	59 mL
½ cup	118 mL
¾ cup	177 mL
1 cup	235 mL
2 cups	475 mL
3 cups	700 mL
4 cups	1 L

TEMPERATURES EQUIVALENTS

FAHRENHEIT(F)	CELSIUS(C) (APPROXIMATE)
225 ℉	107 ℃
250 ℉	120 ℃
275 ℉	135 ℃
300 ℉	150 ℃
325 ℉	160 ℃
350 ℉	180 ℃
375 ℉	190 ℃
400 ℉	205 ℃
425 ℉	220 ℃
450 ℉	235 ℃
475 ℉	245 ℃
500 ℉	260 ℃

WEIGHT EQUIVALENTS

US STANDARD	METRIC (APPROXINATE)
1 ounce	28 g
2 ounces	57 g
5 ounces	142 g
10 ounces	284 g
15 ounces	425 g
16 ounces (1 pound)	455 g
1.5 pounds	680 g
2 pounds	907 g

Appendix 2 Air Fryer Cooking Chart

Vegetables	Temp	Time (min)
Asparagus	375 ℉	4 to 6
Baked Potatoes	400 ℉	35 to 45
Broccoli	400 ℉	8 to 10
Brussels Sprouts	350 ℉	15 to 18
Butternut Squash (cubed)	375 ℉	20 to 25
Carrots	375 ℉	15 to 25
Cauliflower	400 ℉	10 to 12
Corn on the Cob	390 ℉	6
Eggplant	400 ℉	15
Green Beans	375 ℉	16 to 20
Kale	250 ℉	12
Mushrooms	400 ℉	5
Peppers	375 ℉	8 to 10
Sweet Potatoes (whole)	380 ℉	30 to 35
Tomatoes (halved, sliced)	350 ℉	10
Zucchini (½-inch sticks)	400 ℉	12

Frozen Foods	Temp	Time (min)
Breaded Shrimp	400 ℉	9
Chicken Burger	360 ℉	11
Chicken Nudgets	400 ℉	10
Corn Dogs	400 ℉	7
Curly Fries (1 to 2 lbs.)	400 ℉	11 to 14
Fish Sticks (10 oz.)	400 ℉	10
French Fries	380 ℉	15 to 20
Hash Brown	360 ℉	15 to 18
Meatballs	380 ℉	6 to 8
Mozzarella Sticks	400 ℉	8
Onion Rings (8 oz.)	400 ℉	8
Pizza	390 ℉	5 to 10
Pot Pie	360 ℉	25
Pot Sticks (10 oz.)	400 ℉	8
Sausage Rolls	400 ℉	15
Spring Rolls	400 ℉	15 to 20

Meat and Seafood	Temp	Time (min)
Bacon	400 ℉	5 to 10
Beef Eye Round Roast (4 lbs.)	390 ℉	45 to 55
Bone to in Pork Chops	400 ℉	4 to 5 per side
Brats	400 ℉	8 to 10
Burgers	350 ℉	8 to 10
Chicken Breast	375 ℉	22 to 23
Chicken Tender	400 ℉	14 to 16
Chicken Thigh	400 ℉	25
Chicken Wings (2 lbs.)	400 ℉	10 to 12
Cod	370 ℉	8 to 10
Fillet Mignon (8 oz.)	400 ℉	14 to 18
Fish Fillet (0.5 lb., 1-inch)	400 ℉	10
Flank Steak(1.5 lbs.)	400 ℉	10 to 14
Lobster Tails (4 oz.)	380 ℉	5 to 7
Meatballs	400 ℉	7 to 10
Meat Loaf	325 ℉	35 to 45
Pork Chops	375 ℉	12 to 15
Salmon	400 ℉	5 to 7
Salmon Fillet (6 oz.)	380 ℉	12
Sausage Patties	400 ℉	8 to 10
Shrimp	375 ℉	8
Steak	400 ℉	7 to 14
Tilapia	400 ℉	8 to 12
Turkey Breast (3 lbs.)	360 ℉	40 to 50
Whole Chicken (6.5 lbs.)	360 ℉	75

Desserts	Temp	Time (min)
Apple Pie	320 ℉	30
Brownies	350 ℉	17
Churros	360 ℉	13
Cookies	350 ℉	5
Cupcakes	330 ℉	11
Doughnuts	360 ℉	5
Roasted Bananas	375 ℉	8
Peaches	350 ℉	5

Appendix 3 Recipes Index

Made in the USA
Las Vegas, NV
27 December 2024

15435138R00058